Uniting the States

A Commentary on the American Constitution

Third Edition

Lucas Kent Ogden

Printed an published by:
BoD - Books on Demand, Norderstedt
ISBN 978-3-7322-3115-7

CONTENTS

Preface i

1. Introduction to the Constitution

Historical Background 1
The Framers of the Constitution 4
The Constitution and Slavery 8
The Purpose and Structure of the Constitution 11

2. The Bicameral Congress (Article I, Sections 1-7)

One Congress, Two Houses (Section 1) 16
The House and the Senate (Sections 2-3) 17
General Rules for Both Houses (Sections 4-6) 22
Making Laws (Section 7) 27

3. Congressional Powers (Article I, Sections 8-10)

Financial Powers (Section 8, Clauses 1-6) 31
Various Powers (Section 8, Clauses 7-18) 36
Limits on Congress (Sections 9) 41
Limits on the States (Sections 10) 44

4. The President and the Supreme Court (Articles II-III)

Electing the President (Article II, Section 1) 46
Presidential Powers (Article II, Sections 2-4) 51
The Supreme Court (Article III, Section 1) 57
Extent of Judicial Power (Article III, Sections 2-3) .. 60

5. American Federalism (Articles IV-VII)

The States (Article IV) 65
Amending the Constitution (Article V) 68
Constitutional Supremacy (Article VI) 70
Ratification (Article VII) 73

6. **Basic Liberties of Citizens (Amendments I-IV)**

Freedom of Religion (Amendment I, Clause 1)	76
Freedom of Expression (Amendment I, Clause 2)	82
Arms and the Security of a Free State (Amendment II)	84
Security and Privacy (Amendments III-IV)	87

7. **Rights Under the Justice System (Amendments V-X)**

Basic Rights of the Accused (Amendment V)	91
Further Rights of the Accused (Amendments VI-VII)	95
The Imprisoned and Convicted (Amendment VIII)	97
Rights not Mentioned Here (Amendments IX-X)	99

8. **Early Reforms and American Reconstruction (Amendments XI-XV)**

Early Governmental Reforms (Amendments XI-XII)	101
The End of Slavery (Amendment XIII)	103
Equally Protected Citizens (Amendment XIV, Section 1)	107
The Right to Vote (Amendments XIV, XV)	111

9. **The Early 20th Century (Amendments XVI-XXI)**

Power to the People (Amendments XVI-XVII)	114
Purchasing Alcohol (Amendments XVIII, XXI)	116
Voting Rights for Women (Amendment XIX)	120
Reforms in Governmental Procedure (Amendment XX)	122

10. **Further Modifications (Amendments XXII-XXVII)**

Presidential Elections (Amendments XXII, XXIII)	125
Abolishing the Poll Tax (Amendment XXIV)	127
Replacing a President (Amendment XXV)	129
Voting Age and Congress' Pay (XXVI, XXVII)	131

Outlook: Constitutional Law 134

Further Reading 137

Appendix A: The Constitution (text)
  Articles I-VII 140
  The Bill of Rights 155
  Additional Amendments to the Constitution 158
  Unratified Amendments 167

Appendix B: Overview of Amendments 169
Appendix C: Government Comparison 170
Index of Selected Key Terms 172

Preface

After more than 200 years, the Constitution of the United States is still the "highest law of the land" (Article VI). Anyone who becomes familiar with its central principles will not only gain insight into one of the most important documents of democratic government, but will also become much better equipped to understand and to participate in debates about current issues concerning the United States. Of course, due to this country's current status as a superpower with tremendous impact and influence around the globe, the American government's decisions and how it applies the Constitution interest and affect far more people than the citizens it represents.

This concise, readable commentary presents and explains the American Constitution in way that is accessible for a broad audience. Its contents are closely connected with lectures and seminars I have given at the University of Tubingen in Germany. While written mainly for university students without specialized background knowledge about American law, this book can prove helpful for any interested readers (of any nationality) hoping to gain a clearer and deeper understanding of the government's powers and citizens' rights in the United States.

This book's structure closely follows that of the Constitution. Background information is provided in Chapter 1, and Chapters 2-5 cover each section of the original Constitution's articles, which define how the American government works. Chapters 6-7 address the Bill of Rights, the classic document that protects American citizens' liberties as well as their basic rights under the justice system. Chapters 8-10 then discuss further amendments that have been added to the Constitution over the course of American history. Chapter 8 focuses mainly on the 19th century, featuring the end of slavery and the resulting, new framework for understanding constitutional rights, while Chapters 9 and 10 explain developments in the 20th century. Throughout the commentary, the specific sections and "clauses" (i.e., paragraphs) are referenced, so that these can easily be found in the text (cf. Appendix). The most significant changes in this *second edition* are in the more extensive discussion of civil rights as guaranteed in the amendments, which are now handled in five chapters instead of three. Moreover, recent developments are included, in particular the controversy about privacy rights that exploded shortly after the first edition was published earlier this year (see especially under Amendment IV).

Secondary literature that has been helpful to me is listed in the "Further Reading" section. In particular, the CRS Annotated Constitution provided online by Cornell University Law School's Legal Information Institute is recommended for more detailed notes and references to relevant laws and court decisions. I would like to thank the German-American Institute in Tubingen as well as the faculty and students of Interdisciplinary American Studies at the University of Tubingen for their continued support. I would also like to thank Matthew Kellogg of the German-American Institute and Christopher Landes of the history department at the University of Tubingen for their feedback and suggestions concerning this book. As a theologian, my own academic training dealt largely with interpreting texts in their cultural context. This background has proved very fruitful in studying my country's foundational legal text. Furthermore, my work for the German-American Institute in Tubingen and at the university has included many opportunities to represent and explain my home country abroad. I hope that the following explanation of the Constitution will contribute to trans-Atlantic understanding as well.

The men who drafted the original Constitution had to face the challenge of establishing uniform law and order for diverse groups. Several independent states were brought together under a new central government. How can states' rights be respected, while also binding all the states together in one country and ensuring that all citizens' individual rights are equally protected? These kinds of questions guided how the Constitution was drafted and amended, and continue to be asked today. Differing opinions led to compromises between the Constitution's drafters as well as to disagreements between them about how to interpret the document. Since then, the country has continuously struggled through heated political battles and even through a bloody civil war. Today, the nation spans much of the North American Continent (plus Hawaii) and features deep division on many important political and cultural issues.

In the midst of political battles and cultural changes, the Constitution remains an *enduring symbol of unity*. Compared to other peoples with strong democratic traditions, Americans are particularly attached to their Constitution. The British system, which developed as a gradual process, does not have a written constitution. Switzerland's constitution has been changed and replaced a number of times; a completely rewritten version took effect in the year 2000. France adopted a new constitution in 1958, and this in turn has been amended 18 times. The American Constitution, by contrast, was ratified in 1789, and the Bill of Rights was added just two years later. After that, in over 220 years, the Constitution has been amended only 17 times. The fact that the Constitution is so old helps give it an aura of being an almost "sacred" document, a text that Americans believe in and see as central to their identity as a people. A sense of preserving the nation's *revolutionary heritage* and remaining faithful to the Constitution set forth by the *founding fathers* is still very much alive in the American mentality today. This common heritage and respect for the legal system established by the Constitution remains the basis for the ongoing challenge of *uniting the states*.

Tübingen, end of summer, 2013   Lucas Kent Ogden

Preface to the Third Edition

This third edition is essentially an updated version of the second edition. Firstly, I have revised and expanded on the text, both to further clarify questions that have been raised by my students and to update the material to reflect developments in the last two years. Since the second edition was published, Supreme Court decisions as well as social and political developments have already had a significant impact on how the Constitution is now being interpreted. Secondly, this version of *Uniting the States* has been made more user-friendly. At the request of my students, a brief index of selected topics has been added to make it easier to find information, and additions to the appendix help put a broader perspective on Congress as well as on the amendments.

I would like to thank my students at the University of Tübingen for their questions, insights, and interest, which have encouraged me to update the material in this book. In particular, I would like to give a special word of thanks to Pekka Gaiser for designing the cover for this edition.

Tübingen, fall 2015   Lucas Kent Ogden

1. Introduction to the Constitution

In some ways, the common perception of the United States as a relatively young country can be misleading. In fact, Americans not only have a strong sense of national tradition, but also use an older written Constitution than any other country. Whereas European countries' legal foundations typically reflect their 20th century background of being re-built after the Second World War, or after the Cold War, Americans still base their government and basic rights on a document from the 18th century. It was drafted against the background of the American Revolution with the goal of uniting a group of former colonies that had fought for independence together. The "framers," a select group of respected men from different states, developed a blueprint for a new government. Although they failed to address the problem of slavery or to solve the conflicts between the states, the framers managed to establish a Constitution that has endured to the present day.

Historical Background

In the spring of 1776, delegates from several British colonies along the Atlantic seaboard of North America came together to resume the Continental Congress, which had been meeting to decide how to handle the conflicts between the colonies and their mother country. The American colonists, seeing themselves as free British citizens, had longed to be able to send representatives from their colonies to the British Parliament in London. When taxes were imposed with this wish left unfulfilled, many colonists felt that the British principle of "no taxation without representation" was being violated. The British authorities, on the other hand, insisted they had done much to protect the colonists and their rights and that their interests were "virtually" represented in Parliament and taken into consideration. Moreover, as the British had lost both lives and money defending the colonies and securing the trade routes over the

Atlantic for them, they found the Americans' behavior in refusing to pay taxes unfair and ungrateful.

Tensions only continued to escalate on both sides, with both American protests and British attempts to suppress them becoming more aggressive. When colonists in Boston, Massachusetts, finally dumped tea into the harbor rather than paying taxes on it in 1773 (the so-called "Boston Tea Party"), Parliament responded by taking away the right of Massachusetts to govern itself. Alarmed at this heavy-handed treatment, widely perceived as an act of tyranny, Americans in other colonies sided with Massachusetts in its resistance to British rule, and in 1775 the Revolutionary War began. Delegates from all the colonies finally agreed that they would all break away from the British Crown, which they believed had betrayed the liberties and equal rights that they should have had under British law. On July 4, 1776, they formally issued a Declaration of Independence explaining why it was necessary to "dissolve the political bands" held to Great Britain. The best known segment (paragraph 2) proclaims:

> We hold these truths to be self-evident, that all men are created equal, that they are endowed by their Creator with certain unalienable Rights, that among these are Life, Liberty and the pursuit of Happiness.
>
> That to secure these rights, Governments are instituted among Men, deriving their just powers from the consent of the governed…

This declaration goes on to explain that King George III has not respected these rights; instead of basing his authority on "the consent of the governed," he has asserted "an absolute Tyranny over these States." Therefore, the people have a "right" and even a "duty" to free themselves from this oppressive government and to claim their natural, self-evident and God-given rights.

The actual situation was more complicated. It is difficult to harmonize these words about equality and a right to liberty with the fact that their chief author, Thomas Jefferson, like many colonists, owned slaves! Furthermore, many colonists themselves still felt strong ties to Great Britain and were hesitant to embrace a revolution. However, as the British began to assert their authority with increasing aggression, the Continental Congress decided that complete self-government was the only solution. The Declaration of Independence thus proclaimed the thirteen "united colonies" to be "free and independent states." On the one hand, the various states had joined together with a common purpose, but on the other hand each state maintained its own independence. These two aspects of being united and yet distinct are expressed in the name given to this union – "The United States of America."

As the Revolutionary War continued, the delegates put forth a common plan in "The Articles of Confederation and perpetual Union." Once accepted by all the states, this document guided the emerging country through the Revolutionary War and beyond, from 1781 to 1789. The Articles defined the United States as a "Confederacy," with each state keeping its own "sovereignty, freedom and independence" (Article 2). The purpose of this "firm league of friendship" was to mutually help each other maintain and defend their liberty (Article 3). Moreover, each state was directed to send a small group of delegates to take part in Congress every year (Article 5). While a simple majority of the states were needed for many of the union's decisions, particularly important ones required nine states' agreement (Article 9).

Under the Articles of Confederation, the Continental Congress lacked the power to enforce decisions it made, and the states remained more or less autonomous. For example, Congress could request taxes, but receiving them depended on the individual state governments (Article 7). The states were also slow to pay off their debts from the Revolutionary War, and hesitant to let Congress tax them. In addition, the states argued among themselves, e.g., about their conflicting claims to western territories. Another concern was civil unrest. Indebted farmers started an uprising in Massachusetts, causing landowners and creditors to fear a new rebellion. Standing on the brink of economic ruin and divided into independently-minded states, some feared that the union formed after the American Revolution would not last long.

At the time when they declared independence, most colonists identified primarily with their own states and were not ready to think of all these as composing one united country. However, the Confederation's failures convinced more and more Americans that a stronger central government would be necessary. Finally, the Continental Congress officially acknowledged the weaknesses in the Articles of Confederation and called for a convention to revise them. In the course of the year 1787 all states except Rhode Island responded by sending delegates to meet in Philadelphia, Pennsylvania. Instead of merely revising the Articles, these men ended up writing a new document altogether. This Constitution preserved a Congress in which all the states were represented, but now it would be both stronger and more democratic. Decisions would have to pass through two distinct houses of Congress that would keep each one's power in check. There would also be an executive branch of government with the ability to make sure that decisions made by Congress were actually enforced, as well as an independent court system to review the people's complaints. The United States thus developed from a group of separate colonies into a confederation of independent states, and finally into a republic directed by a central government.

The Framers of the Constitution

The Constitutional Convention met from May 25 to September 17, 1787, in the Pennsylvania State House in Philadelphia, the largest city in the United States at that time. Of the 70 delegates appointed, only 55 of them actually came to the deliberations at all, and 29 attended regularly. In the end, 39 delegates signed the new constitution. At the same location, six of them had signed the Declaration of Independence eleven years before, and five had signed the Articles of Confederation nine years before. There were even two men who signed all three documents. The 39 signers of the Constitution who set up the new government's framework are referred to as the *framers*. These men represent a subgroup of the *founding fathers* or simply *founders*, meaning in general those who led the United States along the way from several colonies to an independent country. Perhaps surprisingly, some of the most important founding fathers did not attend the Convention. Thomas Jefferson, the main author of the Declaration of Independence, and John Adams, whose pamphlet *Thoughts on Government* was influential, were on diplomatic duty in Europe. Perhaps some aspects of the Constitution might have turned out differently if these men, who each ended up becoming president, had participated in the debates. Both wanted, for example, to put strict term limits on politicians so that the same people would not be re-elected, and to include a bill of rights from the start.

The framers were prominent citizens with political experience. Almost all of them had been involved in the American Revolution and most had served in the Continental Congress. About half were college graduates, and the other half were self-taught. They were financially stable and influential men, but some had rather humble backgrounds. Some small farmers had been elected as delegates as well, but were poorly represented. Not only would it have been difficult for them to leave their farms to spend a few months attending debates, but they also generally disagreed with the Convention's goals. In fact, many Americans would have rather remained in a loose confederation, and worried that a new government could threaten the liberties that the revolution had been fought for. The framers, however, had become convinced that a strong, centralized government was necessary for the young country to secure its borders, develop its economy and be taken seriously by Europe. They were afraid of the country falling apart into independent states in conflict with each other and incapable of dealing very well with uprisings, Indian raids and international trade. Being educated and experienced, and understanding the complicated nature of politics, diplomacy and economics, the framers considered themselves more qualified than others to determine what kind of government was needed.

Having been written by a rather elite group, the Constitution of course did not represent all Americans' perspectives equally. Moreover, the framers and their families had important personal interests at stake in strengthening a government that would secure their own societal position, property, and business opportunities, and would be able to hinder uprisings. At the same time, it is also believable that they sensed a strong moral responsibility towards their communities and states. Their efforts indicate a desire for a government that would serve the best interests of society as a whole (at least from their perspective), both for their own generation and for many to come. Though the framers made the government significantly stronger than it had been under the Confederation, they were also careful to keep its power – and their own – limited. Despite their shortcomings, the framers did in fact succeed in setting up a blueprint that would guide their country into the coming three centuries and serve as a basis for it becoming a major world power and a symbol of liberty.

The presence of George Washington of Virginia and Benjamin Franklin of Pennsylvania made the Convention seem very prestigious. Washington, a long-time military officer who led the American forces in the revolution, was seen as a hero throughout the states. In his desire to bring Americans closer together, Washington was ready to accept compromises to strengthen the union. Franklin, at 81 years of age by far the oldest delegate, was perhaps the most famous American internationally. The largely self-educated key figure in trans-Atlantic diplomacy and in the Enlightenment was known as a printer and popular author, as well as for his contributions to science, philosophy and politics. At the Convention, the aged Franklin encouraged respectful discourse among the younger delegates.

While Washington served as the Convention's official president and Franklin played a moderating role, the two framers who actually spoke most often during the debates in Philadelphia were Pennsylvanians Gouverneur Morris and James Wilson. Morris, a polished gentleman from a wealthy, aristocratic family in New York, is regarded as the Constitution's chief drafter. Wilson was a Scottish immigrant and an aggressive land speculator with a turbulent life; his expertise in political theory helped him to be influential in the debates. Morris was hesitant to give power to the common people, being concerned that they could be too easily swayed by money and charismatic speakers, while Wilson spoke out for greater democracy and favored popular elections.

The man who gave the third largest number of speeches in the debates in Philadelphia was James Madison of Virginia, known as the "Father of the Constitution." Of frail health and indecisive about a career, Madison finally got involved in politics. Having spent much of his life on his aristocratic family's estate, and not having been healthy enough to participate in the Revolutionary War, the 36-year old was less experienced than most delegates. As it turned out, however, he was quite brilliant in assessing the exact weaknesses in the Articles of Confederation and laying out concrete plans to build a stronger union. As the main drafter of the "Virginia plan," Madison mapped out a new government with three branches, the law-making branch having two chambers. This was the basic structure adopted by the convention and is still used in the United States today.

The rest of the framers also attended the meetings, participated in the debates and contributed to formulating the Constitution. They represented conflicting interests between smaller and larger states, different opinions about how strong and how democratic the government should be, and were deeply divided about slavery. In the end, the Constitution was a group effort reflecting a long series of compromises, and most delegates were not completely happy with the final document. Under the new government, disagreements continued between the founding fathers, including among those who had signed the same Constitution. When one of the framers, Alexander Hamilton, insisted on creating a national bank, the founding fathers could not agree on whether or not the Constitution allowed this. Congress is not *explicitly* given this power, but Hamilton claimed it was *implied*. James Madison and his mentor Thomas Jefferson emerged as leading opponents of this theory of implied powers. Some framers sided with them, while others supported Hamilton, whose views ultimately prevailed in the first Congress. This development shows that the common question about *what the framers intended* is much too simplistic. If we could ask the framers how to interpret the Constitution they themselves drafted, signed, and defended, we would hear conflicting answers!

The Constitution and Slavery

The most problematic issue that the framers could not agree about was *slavery*. Although *owning* people obviously conflicts with the ideals of liberty expressed in the Declaration of Independence, the original Constitution did nothing to stop it. The southern states in particular would not have accepted a constitution that prohibited slavery. The delegates were trying hard to bring the states closer together. As the slavery problem was too controversial for the Constitutional Convention to realistically solve, it was generally avoided. When it absolutely had to be addressed, then this was done indirectly and with compromises.

Even when slaves are referred to, the embarrassing word is never specifically mentioned. Article IV says a "Person held to Service or Labour" could not gain freedom by simply fleeing to another state, but would have to be returned (Section 2, Clause 3). A central compromise can be seen in the problematic "three-fifths" rule. When determining the total number of citizens in the respective states, "free persons" are distinguished from "all other Persons," who are then each counted as *three-fifths* of a person (Article I, Section 2, Clause 3). The Articles of Confederation had not counted slaves at all and had even specifically mentioned "all white inhabitants" as making up the relevant population (Article 9, Clause 5). By contrast, the Constitution avoided any references to skin color and referred to those held in slavery as "persons." Nevertheless, by allowing people who were not "free" to at least partially be counted among the population, states with many slaves gained a right to greater representation in government.

Almost half of the men at the Convention, including Washington and Madison, owned slaves themselves. Gouverneur Morris, James Wilson, Alexander Hamilton and others opposed slavery. Many from both groups realized how morally problematic and contradictory it was to own people as property in a country proclaiming liberty, though how they personally dealt with this varied. Franklin freed his own slaves, and then as the first president of the anti-slavery society in Pennsylvania helped to abolish slavery in his state. Madison, who owned slaves all his life and could not imagine blacks being integrated into white society, supported the idea of relocating black slaves to a place where they could live free in their own communities. Washington, a life-long slave owner as well, finally freed all his slaves in his will, also providing for their children to be educated.

Many framers hoped that slavery would end gradually, and in fact the early years under the Constitution were marked by progress in this direction. In 1787, when the Constitution was drafted,

Massachusetts was the only one of the thirteen states that had abolished slavery. Under the new government, more states followed in gradually phasing out slavery until the North was dominated by free states. Furthermore, the Constitution protected the slave trade, but only until 1808, when an end to shipping in any more slaves would be possible (Article I, Section 9, Clause 1). This was enacted by Congress in that year, one year after the slave trade had been outlawed in Britain. Unfortunately, as this did not affect people who had already been brought over as slaves or their descendants, the end of the slave trade over the Atlantic did not lead to the end of slavery as many of the framers had hoped it would, but the slave population in the South only continued to grow as ever more black children were born as slaves. In fact, slavery continued a full three decades longer in the United States than in Britain, where it was abolished in 1834. The plan to send slaves back to Africa, which Madison and other founders had financially supported, was not ultimately successful either. In the early 19th century, some freed slaves were relocated to small American colonies on the western coast of Africa, which became the Republic of Liberia in 1847. However, most blacks remained in the United States as slaves, as their masters did not set them free.

As long as slavery existed, the Constitution's ideals of forming a "more perfect Union" and ensuring "domestic Tranquility" stated in the Preamble would be very far off, to say the least. The southern, agriculturally based states continued to cling to this institution as part of their culture, whereas Americans who found it extremely inhumane demanded its immediate end. The states became increasingly polarized, culminating in a civil war, when most of the slave states attempted to leave the union. Abolishing slavery on a national level first became possible after the union victory in the Civil War, and was finally accomplished by Amendment XIII in 1865. The fact that slavery had been tolerated by a document proclaiming the "Blessings of Liberty" and "establishing Justice" shows that the Constitution failed even in its own stated goals.

"Liberty" can hardly mean the freedom to deny others any rights. The very heart of America's revolutionary heritage – *people's rights against oppression* – was denied as long as states were permitted to treat human beings as pieces of property. This inherent contradiction could only be overcome by guaranteeing full rights as citizens to people of all backgrounds. Unfortunately, it would take a long time for the original American vision of freedom to finally reach its logical conclusion.

The Purpose and Structure of the Constitution

In addition to its background and historical situation, the Constitution's own stated purpose and basic structure should be taken into account as well. The document begins with the following famous Preamble:

> We the People of the United States, in Order to form a more perfect Union, establish Justice, insure domestic Tranquility, provide for the common defence, promote the general Welfare, and secure the Blessings of Liberty to ourselves and our Posterity, do ordain and establish this Constitution for the United States of America.

The first words clarify that the authority for governing is derived not from a monarch or an aristocracy, but from the people. The framers do not place themselves above those they represent, but count themselves among them. They thus do not presume any right to set up a new government without making clear that they are doing so in the interest of all the states.

According to the Preamble, the intention behind creating a government in the way laid out in the Constitution is to build a unified country with an enduring commitment to the ideals of justice and liberty for its citizens. This purpose includes six aspects.

First of all, the document should help "form a more perfect Union" by laying out a plan for bringing the states together. By "Union," more is meant here than a "Confederacy" of independent states. A centralized government with the power to make laws for the whole republic and direct its affairs is demanded. The goals that follow have to do with ensuring a *stable system of law and order*. In order to "establish Justice" and "insure domestic Tranquility," an executive branch that enforces laws, as well as a reliable court system that can review people's complaints, will be necessary. This kind of stable, functioning government accountable to the people can then "promote the general Welfare." Furthermore, a centralized military headed by a commander-in-chief serves the interest of the "common defence," helping secure the union against potential wars. Finally, the "Blessings of Liberty," specifically, political liberty for the American people to govern themselves, must be secured by a government based on representation and with limited powers so that it cannot oppress its people. In the hope that this system would endure for many generations to come ("...and to our Posterity..."), the Constitution would have to be written with care and there would have to be a clear way to amend it in the future.

A comparison of the Constitution's Preamble with Article 3 in the Articles of Confederation, written ten years before, is revealing. The purpose is no longer simply for states to offer support and friendship to each other, but "to form a more perfect Union." This idea of binding the states closer together into one united country had become more acceptable than it had been a decade before. At that time it was the *states* that entered "into a firm league of friendship" in the interests of "the people of the different States" (Articles 3-4), but now the delegates speak as representatives of the *people* with one voice as a collective group – "We, the people of the United States." Again, while the Articles of Confederation mention the "liberties" of each of the *states*, the Constitution has a collective focus on "the Blessings of Liberty to ourselves and our Posterity," with "ourselves" referring to all Americans together.

The Preamble portrays the American people as one collective group, speaking of their "general Welfare," the common good. A loose confederation of separate states seeking their own interests had led to economic and social instability. The framers had to compromise both their own wishes and those of their own states in order to draft a document that could be accepted throughout the union. The Preamble does not promote a vision of individuals each pursuing their own goals. Instead, it calls upon Americans to be willing to put aside their own personal interests and even to give up some of their independent states' rights under the Confederation for the sake of forming "a more perfect Union." The reality, however, fell far short of this vision of unity. People's primary loyalty was still to their respective states and many did not like a central government interfering. Within a century several states would finally try to leave the union and to form a new Confederacy of independent states. It was not until the pro-union forces won in a bloody civil war (1861-1865) that the authority of the Constitution and the enduring nature of the union were asserted once and for all. Only after this point was the original usage of the plural for the "United States" gradually replaced by the singular form ("the United States *is*," instead of "are"), reflecting that the states together compose one nation.

The text following the Preamble consists of two major sections. There are seven *articles* ratified on March 4, 1789, and then there are 27 *amendments* that have been added since. The articles lay out the basic structure of the American government, defining how it works and what its powers are. The first article makes up about half of the original text and is concerned with Congress, the government's law-making branch. After that, six shorter articles deal with additional questions about governmental power, such as ones regarding the president and the courts. The articles define the government's power, but not the precise rights of American citizens. The first ten amendments were added as a group shortly afterwards, obtaining official status in 1791. This "Bill of Rights," which is enshrined in the National Archives Building in Washington, D.C. along with the original Constitution, is held in particularly high esteem by the American people.

Finally, seventeen further amendments have been added to the Constitution throughout the course of its history. These have modified how the government works and specified what rights people have. In the amendments, the original Constitution's most problematic aspects (from a modern perspective) are corrected. Judging by 21st century standards, we may be rather shocked or upset that the framers did not give the people a fundamental right to vote, nor did they eliminate slavery. Racial and ethnic minorities, women, and even poor white men were not yet represented in the way we would expect and demand today. Men were thought to represent their families publically, wealthy gentlemen were considered fitter to govern than the common masses, and whites often assumed that non-whites were somehow less intelligent than they were and best suited to low-level labor.

Although the founders held certain concepts prevalent in the 18th century that are no longer acceptable today, by the standards of that time, they took a decisive step forward in several respects. The Constitution set up a government of the people in which no positions of authority were gained as a simple birthright; there was no monarch or inherited aristocracy. Political ideas that had been discussed in Europe were now tried out for the first time. People in different regions could vote directly for representatives, and had many opportunities for democratic involvement in their own communities, regions and states. Citizens were guaranteed many basic rights and liberties that could not be taken for granted at that time. Of course, the Constitution has never been a perfect document, and was even used to support slavery and racial segregation. Nevertheless, it has proved flexible enough for future generations to add appropriate amendments and accept new laws so that the *ideals of liberty and justice* can be more fully realized. Furthermore, the fact that the American Constitution has endured so long in spite of dramatic changes in society testifies to its strength. To this day, despite serious division and conflict in America's cultural and political landscape, the Constitution still holds the nation together, continuing to *unite the states* in the legal tradition they all have in common.

As already noted, it is important to keep in mind that the framers, as well as the founding fathers in general, were sharply divided among themselves on many major political issues of their own time. Even those who had signed the same Constitution did not always agree with each other about how exactly it is supposed to be interpreted and applied in concrete situations. Moreover, the framers did not draft a book of answers settling any political questions once and for all, nor did they proclaim an elaborate series of timeless rules that can never be re-interpreted or modified. Rather, the framers established guidelines that are supposed to give future generations the ability to decide *for themselves* how to deal with the political questions of their own day without the repressions of tyranny. Furthermore, the Constitution does not necessarily guarantee that the decisions made under this framework by future generations will be "right" or beneficial to society as a whole, but it gives them the *freedom* and the moral *responsibility* to do so.

2. The Bicameral Congress (Article I, Sections 1-7)

The Constitution's plan for the American government divides power between three distinct branches: legislative, executive, and judicial. The legislative branch makes laws, the executive branch enforces ("executes") them, and the judicial branch listens to people's complaints and passes judgment. The legislative, i.e., "lawmaking," branch is called *Congress*, corresponding to Parliament in Britain. In Congress, originally thought to be the most powerful branch, power is again divided between *two separate chambers* or "houses." In each of them, people representing their respective states come together to make laws for the whole country. Article I describes the structure and powers of this *bicameral* ("two-chamber") body, taking up most of the first two pages of the original four-page Constitution. The first seven sections focus on how Congress is formed and how it operates.

One Congress, Two Houses (Section 1)

From 1781 to 1789, under the Articles of Confederation each state could send a delegation to Congress. Much of the debate at the Constitutional Convention in 1787 centered around how to reform this body. The smaller states wanted each state to continue being equally represented in Congress. Otherwise, they feared, the larger states would dominate government. The larger states, however, insisted that it was only fair for states with higher populations (i.e., more taxpayers) to have more representatives in Congress than smaller states. In the end, the framers agreed to what is known as the "Great Compromise" – *both* plans would exist parallel to each other. The *House of Representatives* would be based on population, and in the *Senate* all states would be equally represented. As a further part of the compromise, representatives would be elected directly, while senators would be appointed by state governments.

Together, the House and the Senate make up the two chambers of the bicameral United States Congress, which according to Article I, Section 1, has "All legislative Powers" that are given in the Constitution. Congress alone can make new laws in the United States. On the other hand, as neither chamber can do so on its own without the other's approval, *the Senate and the House of Representatives keep each other in check*. In addition, Congress is kept in check by the president, who can stop laws from being passed, and by the Supreme Court, which can strike laws down. This plan is based on *checks and balances* and a *separation of powers*.

Many other countries also feature a bicameral system of an upper and a lower house. One of the traditional ideas here is that an upper house, made up of experts who are not campaigning for the next election, can keep the lower, more populist house from making popular but problematic decisions. The British House of Lords is a classic example of an aristocratic upper house in which positions are (at least have been traditionally) inherited or appointed by the monarch. Depending on the country, upper houses might be elected by state legislatures (the Netherlands, Austria, India), or by government officials (France, Ireland, Russia). They may even simply be appointed by state governments (Germany, European Union), or by a single federal governmental leader (Canada). In some countries, the majority of seats in the upper house are elected directly, while a minority are appointed (Spain, Italy, Belgium). Other bicameral countries let the people elect all the seats for both houses directly (Australia, Mexico, Switzerland, Poland). The United States joined this latter group in 1913, representing in many eyes a strengthening of popular democracy.

The House and the Senate (Sections 2-3)

Section 2 lays out the basic plan for the House of Representatives, and Section 3 for the Senate; to a certain extent these two sections parallel each other. There are three corresponding qualifications for members of both houses (Section 2, Clause 2; Section 3, Clause 3). (1) The minimum age is 25 for representatives, and 30 for senators. (2) Representatives have to have been American citizens for at least seven years, and senators for at least nine years. The differences in these requirements reflect the idea of the Senate being more senior. (3) All elected members of Congress have to actually live in the state they are elected in. As nothing is said about how long they must have lived there, they can originally come from another state or even from another country.

Section 2, Clause 1 clarifies that the House is elected completely anew every two years. Who exactly could participate in elections was originally a matter left up to the states. Women, blacks, and even white men without property were not necessarily included in the democratic process. The rule is that whoever can vote for the largest house of their own state legislature (which originally differed from state to state) has to also be allowed to vote for representatives in Congress. Later, amendments were added to give all citizens voting rights and to outlaw voting discrimination due to race or sex (XIV, XV, XX). In 1789, even limited democratic elections for the House of Representatives were something new, and, as in any country, it would take some time for democratic institutions to develop further.

The number of representatives depends on population, which is determined by a census ("Enumeration") taken every ten years (Section 2, Clause 3). Congress is empowered to regulate this, ensuring that the same standards are used to measure population throughout the states. The two rules mentioned here are that each member of the House represents at least 30,000 people, and each state gets at least one representative (no matter how small the population). The original number of representatives for each state is then listed, ranging from one representative each for the small states of Rhode Island and Delaware, to ten for Virginia. Today, several states have one or two representatives, while the most populous states have very many, the largest group being the 53 representatives from California. The population having grown tremendously since the founding period, today each representative represents over 20 times (!) more than the minimum requirement of 30,000 people. States divide themselves up into regions, or "districts," letting each district choose its own representative.

Having a census to determine representatives forced the framers to address some controversial issues. In particular, would slaves be considered part of the population? What about servants, ethnic minorities, or American Indians? Section 2, Clause 3, attempts to answer these questions by assigning representatives according to the population that can be counted for a "direct Tax" (i.e., based directly on population and/or property) paid by the states to the federal government. The more people that the government can *tax* a state for, the more representatives that state has a right to. People bound to limited terms of service were included for taxes, so they were also included for representation purposes, whereas Indians living within state borders but not paying taxes were explicitly excluded.

This reasoning is at the heart of the compromise on slavery as well. If the federal government was permitted to tax states for their slaves (for "all other Persons"), then slaves could also be counted for representation purposes. As states with large slave populations wanted to get more representatives, and the other states wanted them to pay more taxes, both sides agreed to include slaves. However, to avoid putting them on an equal footing with citizens, *three-fifths* were taken into account. For example, one citizen with ten slaves would be counted as seven people. Once slavery was finally made illegal by Amendment XIII in 1865, this rule about so-called "all other Persons" was nullified. On the other hand, the principle of "no taxation without representation," which had already been a central demand before and during the American Revolution, still stands for an enduring legacy guaranteed by this clause. In the same vein, American territories (e.g., Puerto Rico) do not have representatives or senators, and accordingly do not pay federal income tax.

In contrast to the House, the Senate did not require dealing with questions about population or elections. Regardless of population, each state has always sent two senators. As states have been added to the nation, the Senate has grown to the current total of 100. Moreover, the Senate was originally conceived of as a semi-aristocratic body of level-headed officers appointed by state governments to keep the popularly elected House in check. Congress was obviously influenced by the model of the British Parliament, which itself already had two houses. The House of Representatives corresponded to the British House of Commons, and the Senate to the House of Lords. Although this basic structure remains, extending popular elections to the Senate as well since 1913 (Amendment XVII) has meant that the difference between the bodies is no longer as great and that state governments are no longer represented in Congress.

An additional difference between the House and Senate is that the latter's membership is more stable. While the entire House is up for re-election every two years, senators remain in office for six-year terms and are divided into three "Classes" (Section 3, Clause 2), one of which is up for election every two years. Even today, every two years, American voters elect the *entire* House of Representatives and approximately *one-third* of the Senate. When public opinion sways, the House can change more rapidly than the Senate can. At least in this way, the Senate still fulfills the framers' intention of keeping the more populist House from making rash new decisions based on fluctuations in public opinion. If the people really want to enact major changes in the government and laws, it is possible to elect a much different Senate as well, but this will take more time. An example of this distinction between the two houses can be seen in connection with the health care reforms passed by Congress in 2010. A wave of public opposition to the reforms resulted in a new, more critical House of Representatives being elected. However, the

House was not able to undo the health care reforms that had already passed because the Senate still supported them.

In addition to the basic make-up of the House and Senate and qualifications for their members, a few further issues are addressed in parallel in Sections 2 and 3. If "vacancies happen" in the seats available for representatives from any state (i.e., if a representative dies, resigns or is removed), then that state's governor is required to "issue Writs of Elections," meaning to call a special election so the people can vote to fill the position (Clause 4). For vacancies in the Senate, governors were allowed to "make temporary Appointments," while the state legislatures were responsible for choosing longer-term replacements (Clause 2). In 1913, Amendment XVII changed this so that vacancies in the Senate are now dealt with like those in the House.

Furthermore, each house has an undefined group of "Officers" that it can choose itself. The only positions mentioned specifically are the "Speaker" of the House of Representatives, and the "President pro tempore" of the Senate (Clause 5 in each section). The precise duties of these leadership positions are left up to each house to determine for itself. Each has several committees specializing in different areas of law. The Senate's President pro tempore (by tradition the member of the majority party who has been in the Senate the longest) is actually the back-up leader. The vice president holds the official role of leading the Senate, but, being part of the executive branch, does not actually vote. The one exception is if exactly half the senators vote for and the other half against something, in which case the vice president may cast a vote to break the tie.

The final issue addressed in both Sections 2 and 3 is that of *impeachment*, the process of removing government officers from their positions. The House has the power to impeach the president or any other federal officer (Section 2, Clause 5), but the Senate has "the sole Power to try all Impeachments" (Section 3, Clause 6). A *two-step process* is set up. To be removed from office, a federal official must first be found guilty of "Treason, Bribery, or other high Crimes and Misdemeanors" (Article II, Section 4) by the House of Representatives. Second, the Senate must review and "try" this impeachment, and agree with a two-thirds majority that the official should in fact be removed (Section 3, Clause 6). It is thus possible, but certainly not easy, for this to happen, so that federal officials will be removed only in very serious cases and not due to mere political opposition. If a president is being tried before the Senate, the chief justice (the honorary senior judge) of the Supreme Court leads the proceedings, thus involving another branch of government to help keep Congress in check. Finally, there are three consequences for federal officials impeached by the House and removed by the Senate. First, they lose their current office, and second, they can never hold any public office or title again. The language "any Office of honor, Trust or Profit" covers any government position whatsoever that includes being honored, taking any kind of responsibility for the public, or being paid anything. Third, impeached officers can then be tried by a court and punished for their actions; Congress cannot impose a penalty itself, because that is the court system's responsibility.

General Rules for Both Houses (Sections 4-6)

Section 4 addresses congressional elections, putting the details about "Times, Places and Manner" in the hands of each state legislature. This rule is in the interests both of the states, which can generally run their own elections without federal interference, and of the federal government, which does not have to be responsible for elections across the country. Congress can make uniform laws that affect congressional elections in terms of "Times, Places, and Manner," without changing the basic rules specified in Sections 1-3. "Times" refers to the specific date and time of an election; elections must of course be held every two years for representatives and every six years for senators. Section 4 also says that Congress has to meet "at least once in every Year." This very minimal requirement shows that the framers did not originally envision representatives and senators spending most of the year in the capital or being able to travel as quickly and easily as they can today. It was originally assumed that members of Congress would live primarily in their own states in close connection with the people there, while travelling to vote on laws would be a major event covering only a short part of the year. Since then, the country and its government have grown, and the modern House and Senate discuss, draft and vote on potential new laws all year long. The original date set in Section 4 for a mandatory meeting of Congress, the "first Monday in December," was later moved by Amendment XX to the beginning of January.

Section 5 puts the general rules of how Congress operates into the hands of each house. They are responsible for dealing with questions regarding whether their own members were legitimately elected or are properly qualified. Each can also "determine the Rules of its Proceedings." This means that the Senate and the House each decide for themselves how and when exactly to conduct meetings and discuss and draft potential laws. They each decide what committees they want to have to specialize in writing different kinds of laws. This protects the internal rules agreed on in the House or the Senate from being challenged or changed by anyone else (such as the president), or even by the other house. Each body's independence is protected to maintain a separation of powers. Furthermore, the House and the Senate can each "punish its Members for disorderly Behavior," and can even "expel" or remove members if two thirds agree to this. Again, this protects Congress by making it responsible for its own members. Neither the president nor the courts have the power to expel members of Congress or declare them unqualified. Congress can remove the president and the judges, but this does not work the other way around. Congress was given more trust because it is more directly accountable to the people and the states.

In order "to do Business," i.e., to pass a bill, *over half* of the members in the respective house need to be present. This minimum number is called a "*Quorum*." This requirement ensures that laws cannot be made by only a small minority's support. However, some issues such as drafting laws in a committee can be done by smaller groups. If members of the Senate or the House want to do business but cannot reach a quorum, then they can demand more members to come and can even punish the others for not being there. Once again, the details and exact rules here are left entirely up to each house, in keeping with each of their status as an independent body.

The third clause of Section 5 requires each house to "keep a Journal of its Proceedings" and even to publish this, thus keeping Congress accountable to the public. Nevertheless, Congress can decide to keep some parts secret. Moreover, the specific votes (yes or no) of each representative or senator do not necessarily have to be listed, but will be if *one fifth* of the members present desire this. Even a relatively small minority of Congress members can make sure that the states can see how exactly they and their colleagues voted on specific issues, helping hold members of Congress accountable to the people in their states.

The fourth clause of Section 5 adds that each house needs the other's permission to "adjourn," i.e., stop meeting, "for more than three days." It is not surprising that the Senate and the House often take breaks for two or three days. This rule only applies during the period of the year in which Congress is meeting, called a "Session," which in modern practice is almost for the entire year. Each house also needs the other's permission to meet at "any other Place than that where the two Houses shall be sitting." This requirement also makes clear that both the Senate and the House have to meet at the same location, but the Constitution does not specify where this is. The first Congress under the Constitution started meeting in New

York City, and then moved to Philadelphia. Since 1800, Congress has met in the District of Columbia (cf. under Article I, Section 8, Clause 17).

Article I, Section 6 guarantees all members of Congress "a Compensation for their Services." Under the Confederation, they had been paid by their own state legislatures, meaning that pay could vary significantly from state to state, and even that states could stop paying them if they did not vote in the way that the state legislature wished. The Constitution, however, changes this so that senators and representatives are paid out of federal funds as determined by federal law made by Congress itself. This ensures that nobody (i.e., state governments) can pressure members of Congress to vote a certain way in order to keep their pay. In addition, all members of Congress are given special protection while their house is in session, and while they are travelling to or from a meeting of Congress. Specifically, they cannot be interrogated or brought to court for anything that they say or argue before Congress. They can "not be questioned" about their words "in any other Place" than in their house meeting by their colleagues. These restrictions protect representatives and senators from citizens who disagree with their positions, and who may try to take them to court on the basis of something they said in Congress. This also means, for example, that a president or governor does not have a right to take a Congress member to court for making comments that unfairly damage their reputation (defamation). Members of Congress are not, however, otherwise given immunity from being arrested for breaking the law, specifically in cases of treason (betraying the country), felonies (crimes), and "Breach of the Peace." These have been broadly interpreted by the courts to include any criminal charges.

The second clause of Section 6 prohibits representatives and senators from accepting any government offices that were either newly created or given a pay raise during their time in Congress. If Congress does one of these things, none its own current members can take that position. In addition, no one can serve as a member of

Congress and as an officer for the executive branch at the same time. This ensures that senators and representatives are not controlled by the president, again in keeping with the framers' insistence on a separation of powers. Senators and representatives are allowed to accept offices in the executive branch as long as these already existed before they were in Congress, the salary for the position has not been raised, and they resign from Congress. It is in fact common for presidents, vice presidents and cabinet members to come from the Senate.

The Constitution does not say anything about political parties. Despite the first president George Washington's opposition to the idea of parties, they soon formed among the founding fathers and have been a central component of American politics for most of the country's history. Although there are no limits to the number of political parties in theory, in practice the two party system has firmly established itself. Neither house of Congress has made rules favorable to forming coalitions between different parties, as done in many countries, thus making it very difficult for smaller parties to gain influence. In some ways, both major parties can be seen as unofficial coalitions between different interest groups. While the Republican party is more "conservative," and the Democratic party more "liberal," the reality is more complex. There is a spectrum of viewpoints within each party, and some may be "conservative" in some regards but more "liberal" in others, depending on whether the issue is economics, foreign policy, family law, states' rights, etc. On questions such as marijuana legalization, privacy rights and surveillance, and specific cases of military action, both parties find themselves divided, meaning that like-minded Democrats and Republicans will join together against others from both parties. Moreover, groups that disagree with their own party's positions are often more likely to try to start a movement within their party rather than joining another party or starting a new one. For example, the "Tea Party," named after the Boston Tea Party of 1773, is a conservative movement within the Republican Party promoting traditional ideas about a small and less powerful federal government. It has repeatedly come in conflict with Republican leaders who are willing to reach compromises with the Democrats and who seek a more moderate course.

Making Laws (Section 7)

Under the Articles of Confederation, reaching an agreement between nine states (a majority of two thirds) often proved to be a difficult task. The Constitution lowered the requirement to a simple majority of over 50 percent of the representatives and of the senators. On the other hand, by requiring decisions to pass through both houses, decisions could not be made *too* easily either. Section 7 explains how this law-making process works. Potential laws, which do not (yet) have any legal authority, are called *bills* (a word that can have other meanings in different contexts). The first clause allows either house of Congress to propose amendments to the Constitution or bills on any subject, with one exception – only the House of Representatives can propose "Bills for raising Revenue." This rule corresponds to the close link between *taxation and representation* seen in Section 2, Clause 3. As the number of representatives from a state is closely connected with the number of its taxpayers, it follows that the House should assume primary responsibility for raising taxes.

In any case, no bill can become a law unless *both* the Senate and the House approve of it. As mentioned in Section 5, they can only vote on a bill if over half their members are present. If over half of those present approve, then the bill has passed in that house. Once this happens, the bill is sent to the other chamber. Bills can be repeatedly sent back and forth, e.g., when the House and the Senate have difficulty reaching an agreement about a bill's exact contents or wording. The process can be particularly challenging when the two houses are each controlled by a different majority party (one by the

Republicans, the other by the Democrats), a situation that is not unusual in the United States. When this happens, the support of "moderate" members of Congress who do not always vote with their party can be the deciding factor. Unlike the parliamentary systems of many countries, in the United States party discipline cannot be exercised in a way that demands members to vote together on bills. For Americans, politicians' freedom to vote against the majority of their party confirms that their primary loyalty is not to their party leadership, but directly to the people they represent in their state and/or region.

The second clause of Section 7 introduces an additional control for bills to pass through before becoming law. Once approved by both houses of Congress, a bill has to be sent to the president of the United States, who then has three options. (1) He can sign the bill, officially giving his approval. (2) He can reject the bill, sending it, together with his specific objections, back to the house that originally wrote it. The president's ability to stop a bill from becoming law is known as *veto* power, and is intended to hold Congress in check. (3) The president can simply not react to the bill at all, neither expressly approving of the bill by signing it, nor rejecting it. Once a president receives a bill passed by Congress, he has ten days to respond (not including Sundays). In the first and third case, a bill becomes law, either with or without the president's signature. In the second case, after making note of the president's objections and reconsidering the bill, Congress can override the president's veto if a supermajority of *two thirds* in *each* house supports doing so. The names of the members in each house need to be written down with their individual votes; the usual requirement of one fifth desiring this (cf. Section 5, Clause 3) is not mentioned.

The president's veto power (including the *threat* of a veto) can play a major role in politics. Being elected separately from each other, there is no guarantee that the president and Congress will be of like mind. It is not at all uncommon for the president to be from a different political party than the majority in one or even both houses of Congress. Even if Congress is controlled by the president's party when his term begins, it may well lose its majority in the House of Representatives (and possibly even in the Senate) after the president's first two years. Accordingly, the final sentence of the second clause prevents Congress from using a trick to avoid a veto. Congress could conceivably adjourn, or take a break from meeting after sending the president a bill, and then claim that bill should pass because the president did not successfully "return" it within ten days (since Congress was not there to receive the president's return). If Congress attempts to keep a president from vetoing, then the bill is automatically nullified. The exact wording is that a bill is void if the president sends it back and "Congress by their Adjournment prevent its Return." Presidents sometimes try to turn this rule around to make a so-called "pocket veto," intentionally sending a veto on a day when Congress is not meeting. Then the president can claim that because Congress had adjourned and did not *receive* the veto, the bill is dead and the veto cannot be overridden. To keep this from happening, Congress generally makes sure to appoint someone to be able to receive the veto on any day.

The third clause of Section 7 specifies that the process for passing bills also applies in the same way to "Every Order, Resolution, or Vote" that requires both the Senate and the House to approve. This prevents Congress from trying to avoid a presidential veto by claiming that a new rule it passes is not actually a "bill." However, two kinds of congressional decisions remain that are not covered here. As already seen, the president cannot interfere with the internal rules of either house, ranging from how they form committees to their decisions to expel members. Secondly, the president cannot veto a decision to amend the Constitution. If both houses agree on an amendment, this is sent not to the president, but to the state legislatures for approval (Article V).

Some rules, though not demanded by the Constitution, have become firmly established traditions. The committee process, in which bills are first dealt with by officially assigned *committees* in the

House or the Senate before being openly debated, has become an essential feature of how Congress operates. The Senate and the House each have official committees that focus on specific areas of law. A bill must first be approved by the committee responsible for the particular topic before it is discussed in front of the entire chamber. Moreover, the Senate maintains a rule that members may continue speaking as long as they want to until three-fifths of the senators agree to end the debate and finally vote on a bill. This practice, which is not permitted in the House of Representatives, is known as *filibuster*. In the current Senate, if 41 out of the 100 senators disagree strongly with the majority, they can insist that more debate is still necessary, thus preventing a bill from *ever* being voted on. This means it can often be necessary to gain the support of 60 senators in order for a controversial bill to be passed. In 2013, the Senate introduced reforms to stop senators from using filibuster to keep controversial bills from being introduced at all and to keep the president from appointing new judicial and executive officers. For actually passing bills and for approving Supreme Court nominees, however, the traditional possibility of filibuster remains.

In summary, Section 7 sets up a system that makes sure laws cannot be made too quickly without first being seriously considered and surviving potential criticism. To become law, a bill must always pass through *both* the Senate and the House, and must also be given to the *president* for approval. Each of these keeps the others in check so that no one chamber or branch can push a law through on its own without it first being reviewed. Beyond the Constitution's requirements, the traditions of *committees* in both houses and of *filibuster* in the Senate provide additional hurdles intended to make sure that bills are thought through carefully. Finally, even after a law has been passed, it can be judged unconstitutional by the Supreme Court (see under Article VI).

3. Congressional Powers
(Article I, Sections 8-10)

Once the structure of Congress has been defined, Article I goes on to list the kinds of decisions that Congress is allowed to make (Section 8), as well as clear limitations on governmental power (Sections 9-10). As clarified by Amendment X, Congress has *only* the powers specifically given it in the Constitution, and anything not mentioned is left up to the people themselves or the states. The most controversial section of Article I is Section 8. Even the framers themselves disagreed sharply about how to interpret the right of Congress to "make all Laws which shall be necessary and proper" for carrying out powers given in the Constitution (Clause 18). Another particularly controversial issue has been how to interpret Congress' right to "regulate Commerce" (Clause 3).

Financial Powers (Section 8, Clauses 1-6)

The first six clauses of Section 8 deal mainly with issues affecting *finances*, though Clauses 4 and 5 also include some statements beyond this central theme (naturalization, and weights and measures). The right to "lay and collect Taxes" has always been one of Congress' most important powers. As clarified in Sections 2 and 7, states contribute taxes based on population, which also corresponds to representation in the House of Representatives, where tax laws must always begin. Section 9 adds that Congress cannot place taxes directly on people themselves. Congress can demand taxes only under these conditions. It is significant that Congress not only has power to "lay" (i.e., levy) taxes, but also to "collect" them. Under the Articles of Confederation, Congress asked states for tax money, but then had to simply wait for state legislatures to collect it, which they did not always do. Here, however, Congress is empowered to collect money directly from the states. This also applies to "Duties, Imposts and Excises," referring to taxes placed on imports or exports (cf. Section 10, Clause 2), or on specific kinds of goods. In contrast to taxes based on population, these have to "be uniform throughout the United States." That is, no state can be given unfair tax disadvantages.

The purposes that Congress can use tax money for are "to pay the Debts and provide for the common Defence and general Welfare of the United States." These were very serious concerns when the Constitution was drafted. The United States had large debts to pay from the Revolutionary War and needed to bring in more money from the states than had been possible in the Confederation. The second clause goes hand in hand with this right and need by giving Congress power "To borrow Money on the credit of the United States." The Constitution does not give specific reasons for why money can be borrowed, leaving that up to Congress to decide. The specific laws and money needed for the "common Defence and general Welfare," which can be controversial in concrete situations, are determined by Congress as well.

The third clause, known as the *commerce clause,* gives Congress the power "To regulate Commerce with foreign Nations, and among the several States, and with the Indian tribes." Native American tribes are treated here essentially like foreign nations, and Congress has always held ultimate authority both in economic interaction and in making treaties with them (cf. Clause 10). Still today, agreements made between Congress and Indian tribes are valid even if the states in which particular tribes live object. Since 1924, however, Congress has considered American Indians born in the United States to be citizens. Before this time, they were seen as foreign peoples who could not claim constitutional rights. Today, members of Native American tribes essentially have a special form of dual citizenship.

While Congress' power regarding international trade is relatively low-profile, its right to regulate *interstate* commerce can be a highly sensitive issue. Ever since the founding period, there has always been serious contention about how much power the federal government should have, and what issues are in the hands of the states. The first generation argued over a national bank, which finally succeeded, though not without a fight. More enduring was many states' insistence on a right to decide for themselves about slavery, or later, racial segregation. In the end, these issues were decided for the whole nation, partially with reference to the commerce clause (cf. under Amendment XXIV). Since then, the conviction that the federal government needs to take an active role in protecting the rights of minorities has become generally accepted, though the specific limits on what the federal government can do are still hotly debated.

The central controversy here is how to define the terms "regulate" and "Commerce." Does "commerce" refer only to direct buying and selling, or also to things that affect them? Recently, the question has even arisen if "regulating" can include prohibiting states from selling items or even demanding that people buy certain products. Congress has used this clause to justify a wide range of laws, many of which have been challenged in the courts. Moreover, although there is a tendency to link insistence on states' rights with traditionally "conservative" positions, this is not always accurate. For example, permitting gambling and prostitution in Nevada is defended as that state's right. More controversially, efforts to legalize marijuana or physician-assisted suicide represent some states' attempts to assert their right to make their own laws against federal opposition.

In recent years, the nation-wide regulation of health care has been at the center of this debate. Supporters believed that a solution for the whole nation was necessary in order to guarantee health care access for all citizens. Critics of the national health care plan, however, were concerned that the federal government was expanding its power in a way not permitted by the Constitution. In particular, many Americans found the idea rather problematic that the commerce clause could be used to justify a *"mandate" forcing citizens to purchase something* (in this case, health care). In the end, the Supreme

Court decided that the criticism was correct, but it still permitted the national health care plan to be enacted with certain limitations. The federal government could *not* explicitly *demand* that individuals buy health care under the commerce clause, and it would have to let states retain a large degree of control over how to apply health care funds. Congress could, however, enact a health care *tax* on people without health care (cf. Clause 1), thus pressuring them to purchase coverage.

For people in many countries, the whole debate taking place over in the United States seemed rather baffling. Why would anyone be against giving people access to health care? Why would the courts put limits on the government's ability to enact a health care program? It is essential to remember that a general distrust of centralized government has played a role throughout American history. Many Americans are afraid of the federal government exercising too much power, thus threatening the rights of individuals, regions and states to solve their own problems as they see best. For some, a government that can tell the whole nation what it has to do stirs up images of the English kings ruling as tyrants over the colonies. The American Revolution's heritage as guaranteeing the right for people to govern themselves is deep-seated in the general American mentality. The resistance to a national health care plan was not directed against health care itself, but against the federal government expanding its power over an area of law traditionally left up to the individual states and interpreting the commerce clause in a way that let Congress tell citizens what they had to buy. Many other Americans, however, support a centralized health care program. Pointing to the federal government's positive role in helping poor Americans since the Great Depression of the 1930s and in combating racial segregation and discrimination since the 1950s, they believe that government involvement is also a part of the American tradition and is necessary to help solve the people's problems, such as that of many citizens being without health care.

Deviating from the financial focus of the first six clauses, Clause 4 mentions "Naturalization," the process of becoming a citizen. Since 1868, Amendment XIV has guaranteed that people born in the United States are American citizens and all have the same constitutional rights. However, the Constitution does not say anything about all *candidates* for citizenship needing to be treated equally, leaving the rules and procedure entirely up to Congress. Throughout much of American history, Congress made laws restricting certain racial or ethnic groups from becoming citizens as adults, but it finally stopped this practice in 1952.

Although the Constitution never directly gives Congress the right to restrict *immigration* to the United States, this is generally assumed to be implied by the naturalization clause. That is, controlling immigration is necessary in order to control naturalization. The United States has the largest immigrant population of any country in the world. In addition to the very large number of legal immigrants who come into the country each year, there are also millions of residents without official permission. Many people in the United States believe that undocumented immigrants who live and work in the country should be given a legal status, as they can otherwise be unfairly exploited and discriminated against. Others contend that undocumented persons should not be essentially rewarded for entering the country outside of the law, and that this would likely encourage many more illegal immigrants to come after them. In any case, any children born in the United States, regardless of their parents' legal status, are considered citizens (see Amendment XIV). People whose parents brought them into the country as small children and grew up in the United States are in a particularly difficult position, as they may have little connection to the country they were born in, but they do not necessarily have a right to American citizenship.

Moving on, Clause 4 gives Congress power to pass "uniform Laws on the subject of Bankruptcies." That is, Congress can determine the legal options for institutions, businesses, and individuals that cannot pay their debts. The only requirement is that any bankruptcy laws have to be the same throughout the country, not giving any special treatment to certain states. Congress has also established specific courts that deal with bankruptcy cases.

Furthermore, Clause 5 ensures a stable national currency by giving Congress power "To coin money" and to "regulate the Value" of both it and foreign currency. As states are denied these rights (Section 10), currency is thus centralized and made uniform throughout the country. This was thought to be essential for building a strong economy, as it would be easier for states to trade with each other and for the United States to trade with other countries. Moreover, Clause 6 specifically lets Congress make laws to punish people who counterfeit American money. Another issue addressed in Clause 5 is that Congress can determine "Weights and Measures." The purpose seems to be to promote trade, giving Congress power in case differences in measurements were to create problems for buying and selling goods. Today, the government continues to set uniform standards for both the metric system (the standard internationally) and the English system (the older system still widely used in the United States).

Various Powers (Section 8, Clauses 7-18)

Clause 7 lets Congress "establish Post Offices and post roads." Since mail often crosses state borders, it is very reasonable to put this into the hands of the federal government, ensuring that there is a national, well-functioning postal system. The United States Postal Service enjoys a long tradition of exercising a centralized, federal power accepted by the states in the interest of promoting the "general Welfare."

According to Clause 8, Congress can "promote the Progress of Science and useful Arts." As the term "useful" indicates a pragmatic value, it is not surprising that the American government does not contribute to art for its own sake to the extent that many European governments do. Federal support of the arts is controversial, as art is often supportive or critical of particular viewpoints, something many Americans believe government should not use taxpayer money for. Moreover, the framers hardly intended to empower the government to give special financial support to favored artists and scientists. Rather, the means for promoting science and art is here described as giving "Authors and Inventors the exclusive Right to their respective Writings and Discoveries." This is the basis for American copyright law, which intends to encourage individuals to make discoveries that will be profitable for many people, while being assured they will personally be able to financially benefit. Actual governmental institutions promoting sciences and arts are not explicitly foreseen or provided for here, but such were finally created in the mid-twentieth century.

Clause 9 includes the first reference in the Constitution to the "supreme Court." Even before this is established in Article III, Congress is given power to create "Tribunals inferior to the supreme Court." By the present day, Congress has set up an entire system of lower courts responsible for 94 districts throughout the republic, as well as 11 courts of appeal for larger regions, and additional special courts.

As the ocean lies beyond state boundaries, Clause 10 gives Congress direct responsibility to "define and punish" crimes committed at sea. Congress also has this power with regard to "Offenses against the Law of Nations," originally referring to the generally accepted laws and customs regulating relations between (European) countries at that time. This reflects the framers' interest in the United States (as one country) being a respected member in the international community. On the other hand, Clause 10 also implies that the American government has the right to interpret and apply international law. Even when the United States enters international agreements, Congress holds ultimate authority as to how to interpret these and how exactly to enact punishments for breaking them in matters concerning the American government.

Clauses 11-16 deal broadly with Congress' military powers. Clause 11 gives Congress exclusive authority "To declare War," something which it has in fact done only rarely (cf. under Article II, Section 2). In addition, Congress alone can grant the right to seize property from another state that has wronged one's citizens ("Letters of Marque and Reprisal"), a practice derived from older international law and only applied in exceptional circumstances (the last time Congress issued a letter of marque was during World War II). "Captures on Land and Water," implying a war or war-like situation, are also dealt with by Congress. In these ways, Congress (not the states) is entrusted with ultimate authority over national crisis situations.

In Clauses 12-14, Congress is given power to create and support military forces, something it had already done during the Revolution. Specifically, "Armies" and a navy are mentioned here, covering military units on land and at sea. This has been broadly interpreted to also apply to related branches of the military, i.e., the Marines and the Coast Guard. The Air Force was obviously not foreseen by the framers, as airplanes did not exist until the 20th century. Nevertheless, it was created (originally as part of the army) and accepted as implicitly permitted as well. Congress' broad powers to "make Rules" governing the armed forces are balanced by the fact that it cannot actually command them; that is the president's job (cf. Article II, Section 2, Clause 1). Nevertheless, Congress (not the president) makes all the regulations for the military and decides how to finance it, thus keeping the president's military power in check. Furthermore, when Congress gives money to armies, it can be for a maximum of a two-year period. This means Congress has to reconsider the military situation and re-vote about funding at least every two years, thus eliminating the possibility of it funding long-term plans that it cannot change afterwards. If Americans are upset about money spent on war or other military actions, they can vote for a new House of Representatives (elected every two years) that will then be able to disapprove of further spending. Although Congress generally tends to be slow to stop funding when the United States military is involved somewhere, in this way it did for example play a central role in ending the Vietnam War.

Clauses 15 and 16 expand Congress' military powers to include militias as well. These are military units controlled by the individual states and were of central importance in the American Revolution and in the Civil War. Congress can "provide for" the militia being called to serve the country. Again, Congress cannot actually command the militia, but it can give the president this authority; however, it does not have to do so. Congress can allow the executive branch to command the state militias to "execute the Laws of the Union, suppress Insurrections and repel Invasions." It can also allow federal "organizing, arming and disciplining" of the militia. This only applies, however, to militia units actually "in Service" of the nation. Furthermore, states always keep the right to appoint officers and to train the militia themselves, though they have to respect laws made by Congress about how to do the latter. Today, there are two kinds of organized militias in the United States. State militias under the command of their respective state governors are known as "state defense forces" and are maintained in almost half of the states. Congress has given the president power to command the militia of any state to suppress a rebellion or to subdue actions that deny groups of people their rights or prevent the law from being applied. The United States National Guard represents another development out of the state militias. Its members live throughout the entire country and are prepared to protect and serve their state, and also to fight with the national military (even in other countries) if extra troops are needed. (See also under Amendment II.)

Clause 17 gives Congress broad powers to make laws "in all Cases whatsoever" (!) over an undefined "District" with a maximum size of ten square miles (approximately sixteen square kilometers), a space large enough for a city. This area could be given as a gift ("by Cessation") by states and accepted by Congress to "become the Seat of Government of the United States." Clause 17 also allows the government to purchase additional area surrounding this location to use for a wide variety of buildings. Congress has the same direct authority over this purchased property as well.

Under the Confederation, the seat of Congress had moved a number of times and depended on the protection of state governments. It seemed clear that a permanent location under the direct protection of Congress itself would create a more stable position for the new federal government. Having a separate district would also mean that the capital would not be a part of any state, and thus would seem more impartial. No specific location is mentioned in the Constitution, but the plural "states" indicates that the "District" should be formed from land given from more than one state. George Washington, the first president, chose the spot, and Virginia and Maryland agreed to contribute land for this purpose. The area was then increased by purchasing land around it. Since 1791 this location, known as Washington, the District of Columbia, has served as the nation's capital. It includes all branches of government as well as many national monuments, and has also grown into a relatively large city. Not being a state or a part of any state, residents are not represented in Congress (see under Amendment XXIII).

The final clause in Section 8 ended up being controversial from early on. It gives Congress the following authority:

> To make all Laws which shall be necessary and proper for carrying into Execution the foregoing Powers, and all other Powers vested by the Constitution in the Government of the United States, or in any Department or Office Thereof.

Known as the "necessary and proper" clause, this gives Congress power not only to make laws as specifically listed here, but also other laws needed in order to do these things. The point is to make sure that Congress can carry out its powers. Congress has been able to use this clause to make rules organizing the other branches of government beyond what is specifically stated in the Constitution. To this day, the structure of the court system and the executive branch are organized largely according to laws passed by Congress, which helps keep these branches in check as they cannot simply make all their own rules. In some cases, however, it can be debatable if certain actions taken by Congress are really "necessary" or not. The very first Congress under the Constitution was faced with the question of creating a national bank. Some framers believed this was "necessary and proper" to help the government deal most effectively with money. A central financial institution could help it "borrow money" (Clause 2), "support Armies" (Clause 12), and handle tax money responsibly to pay its debts (Clause 1). Others insisted that a national bank – something never mentioned in the Constitution – was not really "necessary" to these ends. Despite strong opposition, Congress approved a national bank and there has been one ever since. Nevertheless, the courts have made sure that Congress cannot use implied powers or the necessary and proper clause in any circumstances it wants, but always needs to show a strong link between making laws and exercising the powers specifically given it in the Constitution.

Limits on Congress (Section 9)

Section 9 lists several limitations on what Congress is allowed to do. The first clause no longer applies today, while the rest are still in force. Clause 1 kept Congress from stopping "The Migration or Importation of such Persons as any of the States now existing shall think proper to admit." This allowed the states to continue bringing in slaves, while such direct wording was consciously avoided. Congress was empowered to take in a small tax for "such Persons" (a morally questionable way of gaining federal money), but this is limited to a maximum of ten dollars per person. However, a time limit was also set – this would all apply only until 1808. Then, Congress would be allowed (but not required) to limit "such Importation." By temporarily protecting the slave trade, the Constitution was more likely to be accepted by states with large numbers of slaves. Opponents of slavery came to accept this compromise as well, believing that they could work on ending slavery in more states and gathering support to end the slave trade once possible in 1808. In fact, they were initially rather successful, reaching both of these goals. Afterwards, however, the abolitionist movement was not able to end slavery in the southern states until Amendment XIII was ratified in 1865.

Clauses 2-6, which are still applicable to this day, limit Congress from taking the following actions:

- Suspending habeas corpus
- Passing a law allowing attainder or ex post facto
- Placing direct taxes
- Taxing state exports
- Privileging ports in some states over those in others

Clauses 2 and 3 are aimed at protecting the rights of people accused of crimes, and include terms inherited from the British legal tradition. The "Writ of Habeas Corpus" refers to a prisoner's right to ask the courts to review if the imprisonment is lawful. In normal circumstances, Congress cannot make any law that even temporarily removes ("suspends") this right. Exceptions can be allowed, however, "when in Cases of Rebellion or Invasion the public Safety may require." When exactly such exceptions might apply can be quite controversial. In 2006 Congress suspended habeas corpus rights for prisoners in Guantanamo Bay believed to threaten public safety, but the Supreme Court ultimately ruled this unconstitutional. Furthermore, Clause 3 prohibits Congress from passing laws either to convict people as guilty of crimes without a trial ("attainder"), or to punish them for actions that were not yet illegal when they did them ("ex post facto").

The fourth clause limits what kind of taxes Congress can demand, ruling out taxes placed *directly* on individual citizens. Congress can of course tax *states* based on the size of their population (Article I, Section 2, Clause 3), requiring that states with larger population pay more taxes (and send more representatives). However, Congress is here forbidden from demanding *individuals* to directly pay the federal government due to their mere existence or having private property. This also meant, however, that Congress would have trouble trying to tax people for property or money earned from interest. Particularly as some parts of the country became increasingly industrial, this clause seemed to give industrialists an unfair tax advantage, and was finally modified in 1913 by Amendment XVI.

In Clauses 5 and 6, the focus shifts from individuals to states, which are also protected from Congress. When states export goods or products to other countries, Congress cannot tax them for this. Congress may regulate trade and tax *incoming* goods, but not in any way that treats states unfairly. No state's ports can be given special privileges, and no state can be forced to pass through or pay at another state's port. These rules reflect the distrust states had of one another and helped settle fears some may have had about a majority in Congress making laws to the disadvantage of a minority of states.

Clauses 7 and 8 are no longer focused on limiting Congress' power, but that of the executive branch. Money cannot be taken from the treasury without Congress first passing a law to allow this for a specific purpose. Moreover, precise records of how "public money" has been spent must be published, so that taxpayers can review exactly what the government has been doing with their money. Finally, Section 9 closes with statements limiting special honors. The government is prohibited from giving any "title of Nobility," e.g., "Sir" or "Lord," that would seem to give some citizens a special status. Though the framers were not necessarily opposed to a semi-aristocratic class (they saw themselves as part of it!), they believed that status should be earned by one's reputation and competence, not inherited or given by the government. Section 9 also forbids anyone who works for the government (given any payment or responsibility) from accepting anything from any foreign government or leader unless Congress specifically allows this. The terms here are all-inclusive to rule out any possibility of the American government being influenced or bribed by other countries.

Limits on the States (Section 10)

Under the Confederation, states printed their own money and in some ways acted like independent countries. Section 10 placed new limitations on the powers of the states "in Order to form a more perfect Union" (Preamble). First of all, it prohibits states from acting as if they were autonomous countries. Becoming part of a "Treaty, Alliance, or Confederation" or granting "Letters of Marque and Reprisal" (cf. under Clause 8, Section 11) are actions that sovereign nations might take in international relations, and are thus put solely the federal government's hands. Moreover, the nation's currency is centralized as well. States are no longer allowed to print their own money, or anything that functions similarly to it (neither "Bills of Credit," nor payment other than simple gold or silver coins without markings). Secondly, states are not allowed to exercise governmental powers that not even the federal government has (cf. Section 9, Clauses 4 and 8). Just like the federal government, states can neither punish people without giving them a trial nor punish them retroactively for something that was not yet illegal when it was done. They cannot "grant any Title of Nobility" either. Furthermore, states are prohibited from making any "Law impairing the Obligations of Contracts." That is, they cannot interfere with contracts made between their citizens by unfairly permitting some people to break them. Basically, just as Section 9 attempts to keep the federal government from becoming overly powerful, the same is done here concerning state governments.

Following the categorical prohibitions in the first clause (things states can *never* do), the second and third clauses of Section 10 add actions that states cannot take "without the Consent of Congress." States can no longer put taxes on imports or exports without special permission. Even then, the tax money gained has to go to the federal treasury, though customs fees ("Duty of Tonnage") can be allowed by Congress without this restriction. An exception is given for states to raise "absolutely necessary" fees to finance the inspection of goods entering or leaving the state. Even these kinds of laws, however, can be reviewed and modified by Congress. States also need permission from Congress to have a military presence beyond the state militia, or for official relations with other states or foreign countries, whether peaceful ("Agreement or Contract") or involving war. The only exception to the latter restriction is when states do not have time to wait for Congress' approval and must react immediately due to "imminent Danger" or actually being invaded. In short, Congress is given ultimate authority over all economic and political dealings that states might have with each other or with other countries. This principle helps maintain the country's clear unity and avoids problems arising between individual states and foreign powers.

Today, states do in fact, with Congress' permission, enter into agreements with other countries. For example, since states issue their own driving licenses, they also decide to mutually recognize driving licenses with other countries. If one American from California and another from Arizona move to Germany, only the Californian will have to re-take driving tests to get a German driving license, as the German government has an agreement with the state of Arizona, but not with California.

4. The President and the Supreme Court (Articles II-III)

In addition to Congress, the Constitution created two new branches of government, the executive and judicial branches, which are each headed by the president and by the Supreme Court, respectively. This completed the system of "checks and balances," in which each branch is elected or appointed separately from the others and keeps the others in check. As a precaution against letting any single branch become strong enough to act tyrannically, power is divided between them and controls are placed on each one. Article II, which has been amended more often and more extensively than any other article, explains presidential elections, powers and duties, while Article III gives brief directions for the Supreme Court.

Electing the President (Article II, Section 1)

Although the Articles of Confederation had demanded states to follow Congress' decisions (Article 13), in reality they could ignore them. While Congress could appoint a "president," at that time this meant nothing more than "one of their members to preside" (Article 9, Clause 5). Going beyond such an honorary role in the older Confederation, Article II of the Constitution foresees a president who holds real "executive Power," the ability to enforce, or "execute," the laws made by Congress. This president is elected together with a vice president for a four-year term. As terms are two years long for representatives, and six years for senators, the president's time in office will never run exactly parallel to the term of any member of Congress.

Section 1, which has been amended twice, describes how the indirect election process works. In contrast to elections for representatives (and later, senators), the Constitution does not envision direct democratic elections for president by popular vote.

Instead, "*Electors*" from each of the states decide who will be president. People holding any federal office are excluded from being electors, who represent only their states and not the current federal government. Otherwise, how electors are chosen is left entirely up to the states. The *number* of electors is determined by simply adding the number of a state's senators and representatives together; as the latter depends on population, the more populous states have more electors. Originally, these ranged from three in Rhode Island and in Delaware to thirteen in Virginia. Today, the most populous state, California, has 55 delegates.

While Article II, Clause 2, says that electors are to be *appointed* by the state legislatures, in 1868 Amendment XIV gave the right to vote "for the choice of electors for President" to all adult males 21 years of age and older, regardless of race or status. In 1920, Amendment XIX extended this right to women as well, whose ability to vote had previously depended on the laws of their own state. Even so, Americans do not have a constitutional right to vote for the president, but rather for *electors* in their states. Article II certainly leaves the impression that electors are free to make their own decisions when they vote for president. This *indirect* system reflects the reservations many framers had towards popular elections. It also avoids the problem of a national election that would be organized and overseen by federal authorities. Presidential elections – like all other elections – are in the hands of the states; in this case, their electors mediate between the people and the federal government.

Today, it is standard practice for Americans to vote for the president by marking the candidate's name, thus leaving the impression that they elect the president directly. Technically, however, they are voting for a group of electors in their state who have promised to vote for a certain presidential candidate, and who were chosen by that candidate's political party. Typically, once it is clear which candidate has won the most votes from the people in a given state (even if by a very small margin), then the electors pledged to that candidate are appointed by their state to vote for president, all casting their votes for the same person. Contrary to popular belief, this "winner takes all" system is not mentioned anywhere in the Constitution, and was not intended by the framers. With the early rise of political party politics, it became popular as a way to ensure that all the electors from a given state would vote for the candidate representing that state's dominant party, and by 1824 it was being used by most states. Today, it is practiced by all states except for Nebraska and Maine, which may split their electors between different candidates. Furthermore, while many states have laws punishing "unfaithful electors" who vote for another candidate, not all states do. There are not many specific rules in the Constitution, as states are expected to solve potential problems in their own election systems themselves.

The third clause of Section 1 lays out how the electors vote. According to the original text, they were supposed to each "vote by Ballot for two Persons" (at least one of those two had to be living in another state than the electors themselves), and then to "make a List" of the total number of votes. Delaware, to give one example, had three electors (appointed according to that state's laws by its legislature), who would each vote for two candidates, making a total of six votes. If all three delegates voted for the same two candidates, then these two would tie with three votes each. It would also be possible for six candidates to each receive one vote. In any case, after making a list of their votes, signing it and certifying it, the electors in each state are directed to send it sealed to the vice president ("the President of the Senate"), who opens the lists in the presence of both houses of Congress.

Once the votes from the electors in the different states are added together, there are three possible outcomes. (1) If over half of the electors voted for a particular candidate, then that person becomes president. (2) If two or more candidates tie, and over half of the electors voted for each of them (electors could originally cast two votes for president), then the House of Representatives decides which one of them will be president. (3) If no candidate receives a vote from over half the electors, then the House chooses between the five candidates (changed to three by Amendment XII) with the most votes. The second and third possibilities have each happened only once, in 1801 and in 1825, respectively. Besides these two instances, there has always been a presidential candidate with enough delegates to win. If the House has to vote for president, its members vote in groups according to state; a majority of the states is needed, and at least two-thirds of them have to participate. The "quorum" is thus stricter than the usual requirement of a simple majority (cf. Article I, Section 5).

In all three cases, according to the original text, whoever had the most electoral votes among the remaining candidates would become vice president; if two or more tied, the Senate would decide between them. This was modified after the third president had been elected. In 1804, Amendment XII specified that electors each cast one vote for president and another one for vice president, distinguishing between these instead of simply voting for two candidates. It also added that a majority of electors would be required to elect the vice president as well. Aside from these important changes, the basic procedure for electing president and vice president remains the same to this day.

After describing the process of how electors vote, Section 1 of Article II continues by setting down some further rules. Clause 4 clarifies that Congress can set the date for the electors to be chosen, and the date for them to vote for president, the latter being the same throughout the country. Moreover, according to Clause 5, to be "eligible to the Office of President," a candidate has to be "a natural born Citizen." This is not defined here, but apparently means anyone who was an American citizen at birth, as opposed to being naturalized, i.e., becoming a citizen later. In addition, eligible candidates have to be at least 35 years old and to have actually lived in the United States for at least 14 years.

The party system, though not mentioned in the Constitution, plays a central role in presidential elections. In the *primaries* carried out *within* each political party, candidates argue very sharply against each other and party members vote state-by-state over a few months. Once a candidate has gained the majority of their party's support, the party tries to unite against the other party. Smaller parties and independent people may (and do) campaign as well, but they lack the influence, networking and resources of the two major parties that dominate American politics. Since 1853, all presidents have been either Democrats or Republicans.

Clause 6 declares that the vice president assumes all the "Powers and Duties" of the president if the latter is removed, dies, resigns or is unable to act as president. (This has happened nine times in American history.) It also gives Congress power to make laws concerning what happens if any of these occurrences apply to the vice president as well. Obviously, it could be a major problem not to have anyone acting as president. Finally, to answer questions not addressed in Clause 6, further specifications were added to the Constitution by Amendment XXV.

Section 1 continues by clarifying that presidents are to be paid for their job, and that the amount cannot be changed during their term. Moreover, presidents cannot receive any extra payment ("Emolument") either from the federal government or from any of the state governments. These rules ensure that presidents cannot be essentially "bribed" by Congress or any state to take a particular action. Finally, Section 1 closes by demanding all presidents to make an "Oath or Affirmation" (see under Article VI) before taking office, saying:

> I do solemnly swear (or affirm) that I will faithfully execute the Office of President of the United States, and will to the best of my Ability, preserve, protect and defend the Constitution of the United States.

While members of Congress are required to swear "to support this Constitution" (Article VI), the presidential oath goes further. As the chief executive, responsible for applying the law, the president must swear to "preserve, protect and defend" the Constitution, even if this means using force. Normally, presidents are sworn in by the Chief Justice of the Supreme Court; they raise their right hand and put their left hand on a Bible, and add the words "…so help me God" after the oath; then they give an acceptance speech. These traditions are standard practice, but are not required by the Constitution.

Presidential Powers (Article II, Sections 2-4)

While Article II's first section has been modified by Amendments XII and XXV, the rest of Article II remains untouched. Its second section lists many specific powers that the president can exercise:

- Direct the military as "Commander in Chief"
- Demand official advice from executive departments
- Issue presidential pardons
- Make international treaties (with 2/3 of Senate)
- Appoint federal officers and judges (with Senate)
- Fill vacancies when the Senate is not in session

As "Commander in Chief of the Army and Navy" (as well as branches of the military added since), the president can define war strategies and give military commands. Congress' approval is not required, so that the president can make quick decisions and react immediately to attacks. However, Congress also serves as a check on the president's power. He can send troops into battle, but only Congress has the authority to officially declare war. Even if a president can get around this requirement by ordering "military operations," these are still dependent on the support of Congress, since it determines to what extent it will *finance* them. Furthermore, although militias are normally under the authority of their respective states, the president can command them if needed – but only if Congress gives him this power (cf. Article I, Section 8, Clause 16). The president's role as commander-in-chief was originally considered important to make sure a well-organized military could protect the young country. As the United States grew into a world power with an ever larger military, American presidents' influence in international affairs became increasingly more significant as well. The central role that presidents have played in commanding military involvement all around the globe goes far beyond what the framers could have dreamt.

Perhaps surprisingly, the last time Congress actually declared war was World War II. Since then presidents have commanded "military operations" that were certainly perceived as "wars" in Vietnam, Korea, Iraq, Afghanistan, etc., but were not officially or legally given this name. In light of presidents' extensive role as commander-in-chief and the difficulty Congress had in stopping the use of military force in Vietnam, in 1973 Congress pushed through the War Powers Resolution. This law represents an attempt to keep presidents from acting too independently of Congress. It requires them to inform Congress of any military force they decide to use and limits military actions to 60 days unless Congress specifically approves of prolonging them.

In recent years, President Obama has sought support from Congress in backing rebels in the ongoing civil war in Syria. While Congress has funded the president's plans to help train rebel forces, it has not approved of his appeals to send U.S. military forces to fight there. The president's announcement in 2012 that the U.S. would become militarily involved in Syria if its government crossed the "red line" of using chemical weapons has to this date not been fulfilled. Though President Obama still could have sent military forces for up to 60 days under the War Powers Resolution, he instead accepted a diplomatic solution.

The second power given to the president in Section 2 is the right to demand advice from the "principle Officer in each of the executive Departments." The Constitution does not define any details about such departments, but the first Congress quickly approved of three executive departments to oversee the treasury, war, and foreign affairs. By today, this number has grown to fifteen departments that together employ over 4,000 people. The *departments* also oversee specific *agencies*, the most well-known being the Federal Bureau of Investigation and the National Security Agency. The heads of the departments are appointed by each president at the start of his term and are called his *cabinet*, forming a group of top advisors in different areas of federal law. Congress has also voted to establish independent agencies that do not operate under any department but are run by their own board appointed by presidents and approved by the Senate. Prominent examples include the Central Intelligence Agency and the National Aeronautics and Space Administration.

In addition, the president can "pardon" anyone convicted of a federal crime, officially forgiving them and reducing or completely removing punishment. This authority only applies to *federal* crimes, and does not give the president a right to interfere with punishments given by any of the *states*. The only limitation for federal crimes is when a federal official has been removed from office (impeached). Unlike most presidential powers, this one cannot be hindered by Congress, but is exercised simply by the president's signature. This power has sparked public criticism when presidents have, for unclear or controversial reasons, pardoned people facing serious criminal charges.

In international affairs, the president acts as the chief diplomatic officer representing the United States. The Constitution says here that the approval of both the president and two thirds of the Senate are required to make treaties with other countries. On the other hand, Congress has passed laws giving the president considerable room to make international "agreements" on his own that do not have the status of an actual treaty. Although not mentioned in the

Constitution, the "Secretary of State," who holds the highest ranking position in the cabinet, also oversees international relations and plays a prominent role in forming and promoting the administration's policies.

The president is responsible for appointing ambassadors to represent the United States in other countries, consuls to support Americans abroad, other such "public Ministers," and judges to serve on the Supreme Court. For all these offices, the president needs the Senate's approval (over 50%). Furthermore, a distinction is made between the most important federal officers and "inferior" ones. The former group, even if not specifically mentioned in this list, must also be appointed by the president and approved by the Senate. Lower-level officers do not require this procedure; Congress can decide who should appoint them.

If federal offices requiring Senate approval (cabinet members, judges, ambassadors and public ministers) are vacant during a period when the Senate is taking a break ("Recess"), the president can simply appoint replacements on his own. Once the Senate starts meeting again, then by the end of its next session (generally about a year later) it can either confirm or reject these "recess appointments." In the latter case, the president must find a new officer whom the Senate will accept. In its early years, Congress could have long breaks, and its members would have to travel some distance to meet. Since today's Congress is made up of career politicians who live in the capital and meet regularly, recess appointments today are often made as political moves rather than out of necessity, with presidents appointing people whom they fear the Senate might not initially approve.

Applying Article II, Section 2, often depends on which specific words are used. Presidents seem to like avoiding requirements for congressional approval (especially by 2/3 majorities) by calling things by another name. Presidents make important "agreements" with other nations while avoiding calling them "treaties," which would require Senate approval. Another example is when presidents appoint diplomatic agents (i.e., "secret agents") without asking the Senate, and justify this by saying that these temporary "agents" are not "public officers." Furthermore, presidents may try to call any break in Senate meetings a "recess" so they can make "recess appointments," while the Senate guards against this by emphasizing that it is taking a break but not an actual "recess."

Following Section 2's definition of the president's powers to command the military, demand expert advice from the executive departments, grant pardons, and make treaties and federal office appointments, Section 3 lists additional powers and duties:

- Give Congress information and recommendations
- Call and dismiss Congress
- Receive ambassadors
- Ensure "that the Laws be faithfully executed"
- Officially install federal officers

The president fulfills the first duty here in two ways. First of all, he gives a "State of the Union" speech every year to both houses of Congress together, describing the nation's current condition and suggesting plans for the coming year. Secondly, the president regularly encourages Congress to make specific new laws that he believes are necessary. However, Congress alone has power to formulate and pass legislation. The president's most significant law-making power is actually a *preventative* one that was mentioned in Article I, Section 7 – the ability to veto legislation.

Next, Section 3 gives the president power to "convene both Houses," directing them to meet "on extraordinary Occasions." The president can even "adjourn" Congress, telling it to stop meeting temporarily and scheduling its next date to meet. The president is only allowed to do this if members of Congress themselves are unable to agree with each other about when to stop and start meeting. To date, this has never happened, perhaps precisely because Congress would never want the president to be able to exercise this right. In addition, the president is expected to receive ambassadors and other official representatives from foreign countries, including other heads of state. In carrying out this duty, whether personally or through executive departments, the president assumes responsibility for all diplomatic relations.

Moreover, the president is required to *"take Care that the Laws be faithfully executed."* Though only mentioned briefly, this is often considered to be the president's central duty, corresponding with the "executive Power" mentioned at the start of Section 1. Beyond this, the responsibility to execute all kinds of federal laws implies a broad range of powers. These are often exercised indirectly through the executive departments; the words "take Care" indicate that the president does not need to enforce laws personally. In extreme cases when people or states refuse to accept federal laws, the president may even command the military to bring the situation under control, as was done to enforce the end of racial segregation. The extent of the president's powers under the "take care" clause depends on Congress, which makes the laws that the executive branch then applies. Congress tends to be especially willing to expand the president's and executive branch's powers in times of national crisis, as it has done more than ever before since the attack on the World Trade Center and the Pentagon in 2001 (cf. under Amendment IV).

The president's power to "execute the Law" and "take Care that the Laws be faithfully executed" is often exercised by giving so-called *"executive orders,"* i.e., official directions to executive departments or officers. Although the Constitution itself does not use this term, the concept is thought to be implied. After all, the president only has real power to enforce laws if he can give some kind of command that has to be followed. As the Supreme Court has sometimes ruled specific executive orders to be invalid for essentially making new laws instead of enforcing existing laws, presidents are generally careful about how they word and justify executive orders, basing them on decisions made by Congress or on principles in the Constitution itself.

The last presidential power mentioned in Section 3 is to "Commission all the Officers of the United States," meaning to officially assign people to federal offices once the Senate has approved of them being appointed. Though also considered a duty that the president is required to do, it seems he cannot be forced to so. When the third president, Thomas Jefferson, simply refused to commission many people to office who had been appointed by his predecessor and approved by the Senate, they were never able to actually receive their positions without this final step (*Marbury v. Madison*, 1803).

Section 4 brings Article II to a close by making clear that the president and vice president can be removed from power if found guilty of treason (cf. under Article III, Section 3), accepting bribes, or committing another serious crime. Two presidents (Andrew Johnson and Bill Clinton) have been impeached by the House of Representatives, but no president has ever actually been removed by the Senate. Although this almost certainly would have happened to President Richard Nixon for giving illegal instructions to government officials in the Watergate scandal, in 1974 he simply resigned from office. Since Nixon had technically not been impeached, once the vice-president Gerald Ford then became president, he was able to officially pardon him.

The Supreme Court (Article III, Section 1)

An essentially feature of the system of checks and balances is an independent court system with judges who cannot be manipulated or intimidated by the other two branches of government. Although working court systems were of course already in place in the colonies before the American Revolution, these had not been united as part of a national legal system. Under the Articles of

Confederation, courts were established only by the authority of their respective states. Article 9 allowed Congress to appoint courts for crimes committed at sea and for "cases of captures," and even to appoint a commission of people from different states to make a final decision on interstate disputes. Article III of the Constitution goes a decisive step further, establishing a single "supreme Court" to decide legal matters for the entire country. In keeping with the Preamble, this high court should help create "a more perfect Union" marked by "Justice" and "domestic Tranquility" by clarifying how to interpret federal law and the Constitution. The first sentence of Section 1 reads:

> The judicial Power of the United States, shall be vested in one supreme Court, and in such inferior Courts as the Congress may from time to time ordain and establish.

Although only one court is required by the Constitution, Congress is also allowed to create lower ("inferior") federal courts under the Supreme Court (as already indicated in Article I, Section 8, Clause 9). How many there should be or how they are organized is not explained – such questions are for Congress to decide. In fact, not many details are given about the Supreme Court itself either. The plural "judges" indicates that a minimum of two is required, including the "Chief Justice" mentioned in Article I, Section 3, Clause 6. By leaving the details up to Congress, the Constitution avoided defining the court system in any way that might be controversial, and it also allows Congress to modify the federal court system by majority vote without requiring a constitutional amendment. Furthermore, the division of powers is upheld by giving Congress power to establish and modify the exact system of courts, and by giving the president power (with Senate approval) to appoint judges to fill the positions (Article II, Section 2, Clause 2).

In its first year, 1789, Congress did in fact establish the Supreme Court, deciding that six judges – one chief justice and five associate justices – should be on it. The number of Supreme Court judges fluctuated repeatedly in its early history, but since 1869 it has remained stable at *nine* members. The first Congress also created judicial districts responsible for each state, assigning inferior courts to each district. The federal court structure has been modified by Congress several times as the nation has grown. Since 1891 it has maintained its current three-level structure, with district courts throughout the country, and courts of appeal responsible for eleven different regions. People can "appeal" to the court of appeal in their region to review a case decided by a lower, district court. Most federal cases are settled on the district or appellate levels; the Supreme Court only reviews cases that it considers particularly difficult and important for the whole nation.

The judges of "inferior" federal courts are appointed by the president with the Senate's approval, just as the Supreme Court is (Article II, Section 2, Clause 2). As usual, if the Senate rejects the president's choice, he has to find another candidate whom it will accept. The Constitution does not list any other formal requirements for federal judges such as legal training or previous experience as a judge. In contrast to senators, representatives and the president, nothing is said about a minimum age or years of citizenship or residency. In theory, it seems the president could appoint just about anybody as long as the Senate approved.

The text of Section 1 continues:

> The Judges, both of the supreme and inferior Courts, shall hold their Offices during good Behaviour, and shall, at stated Times, receive for their Services, a Compensation, which shall not be diminished during their Continuation in Office.

This tells us two things. Firstly, federal judges do not have any term limits, but hold their offices for *life* as long as they display "good Behaviour." What exactly "good Behavior" means is up to Congress to decide. It can remove a federal judge from office, like any other federal official, with a two thirds majority in the Senate (Article I, Section 3). Secondly, federal judges are paid a "Compensation," while the specific amount is left open. Congress decides when and how much money judges are paid, but it cannot reduce this amount in a way that takes effect during a judge's time in office. Hence, no judge needs to fear pay cuts for making a decision that is unpopular with Congress.

Although in earlier times justices of the Supreme Court often served until they died, these days they almost always choose to retire. It is not uncommon for justices to retire sooner or later depending on their opinion of the president at the time. A justice may not want a particular president to choose the justice who will take their place, and may wait for a more conservative or more liberal president to take office before retiring. To date, no judge of the Supreme Court has ever been removed from office.

Extent of Judicial Power (Article III, Sections 2-3)

Section 2 goes on to list the instances when federal courts can decide cases regarding laws or "Equity" (principles of fairness applied in court), including first of all the following situations:

- "all Cases… under this Constitution, the Laws of the United States, and Treasury"
- "all Cases affecting Ambassadors, other public Ministers and Consuls"
- "all Cases of admiralty and maritime Jurisdiction"

The first point here gives the federal courts power to judge cases in which the Constitution or laws made by Congress apply. This also means that they can nullify state laws that do not agree with higher, federal laws, or with the Constitution (cf. Article VI). As amendments have been added guaranteeing personal liberties, the number and scope of cases appealing to the Constitution have increased considerably. All cases that arise regarding laws passed by Congress are national in scope and can hence be heard by a federal court. The same applies to the Treasury, i.e., the federal government's financial revenue and resources. For example, Congress has established special federal courts to hear bankruptcy cases. Furthermore, as officials such as ambassadors (representing the government to other countries) or consuls (supporting American citizens in other countries) are directly accountable to the federal government, issues "affecting" them – whether or not they are a party in the case – can be heard directly by a federal court. As cases dealing with events that happened at sea ("admiralty and maritime") are not clearly under the authority of any particular state, these are heard by federal courts as well. In addition, federal courts are to hear "*Controversies…*"

- "…to which the United States shall be a Party"
- "…between two or more States"
- "…between a State and Citizens of another State"
- "…between Citizens of different States"
- "…between Citizens of the same State claiming Lands under Grants of different States"
- "…between a State, or the Citizens thereof, and foreign States, Citizens or Subjects"

Whereas the first three kinds of controversies have to do with *subject matter*, these latter six categories focus on *the participants* or "parties." When a government and/or more than one state or country is involved in a dispute, then the federal courts assume responsibility. The federal government cannot be brought before one of the lower, state courts; at the same time, this makes clear that the United States government itself can be challenged in federal court. In the rest of these situations, more than one state (or country) is involved. If these kinds of controversies were left up to the state courts, disputes would arise about which one of the states should hear the case, and there would be concern about prejudice against parties from other states. It makes sense, then, that the federal courts would step in to decide between the citizens and/or governments of different states. Likewise, it is fitting for the federal courts to handle cases with an international scope, as the states are not independent countries.

After the Constitution had been accepted, public opinion soon turned against the third and sixth of these latter cases, as many Americans did not want foreigners or citizens of other states to be able to force their state to appear before a federal court. These two lines did not last long, but were nullified by Amendment XI in 1795. The fifth clause, which refers to land claimed by different states hoping to expand their own territory, became almost immediately outdated. From the start, Congress itself took control over disputed western areas, silencing states' claims to them, and admitting its territories as new states (cf. Article IV, Section 3). In this list of six kinds of controversies, only three – those involving the United States government, "two or more States," or "Citizens of different States" – are still relevant.

Once the types of cases that the federal courts will hear have been listed, Section 2 divides them into two kinds of "jurisdiction" or legal responsibility. If a case goes *directly* to the Supreme Court, this is called *original jurisdiction*, and if a case is first heard by an inferior court and may possibly be reviewed by the Supreme Court, this is called *appellate jurisdiction*. The Supreme Court has original jurisdiction over two categories of cases – those that have an effect on people in positions appointed by the president ("Ambassadors, other public Ministers and Consuls"), and all cases in which a state government is a party. In all other cases listed here, including those against the federal government (!), parties first go before a lower court, and then they can "appeal" to the Supreme Court to review the decision. In the three-level system in place since 1891, the "courts of appeal" represent an intermediate level between lower courts and the Supreme Court, keeping the latter from being overwhelmed. Congress can decide to make exceptions to the general rule, sending some cases directly to the Supreme Court that would normally fall under its appellate jurisdiction. Congress cannot, however, make laws giving the courts entirely new kinds of powers, as was clarified by the Supreme Court itself in 1803 (*Marbury v. Madison*).

The third clause of Section 2 guarantees that American citizens accused of crimes have a right to a trial by *jury*, meaning fellow citizens decide whether or not they are guilty. This jury trial must take place in the same state where the crime occurred. Beyond these rules, two exceptional situations are mentioned. First, if a government officer is removed from office, then the decision is made not by a jury, but by Congress. Second, if citizens are accused of crimes that were not done in any state – e.g., in a territory of the United States or at sea – then they still have a right to a jury trial, and Congress can make laws determining where the trial will take place. The basic right to a jury trial will be further defined in Amendments V, VI and VII.

The third and final section of Article III deals with "treason," that is, betraying the United States. This exceptionally serious crime was already mentioned as the first reason why a government official can be removed from office (Article II, Section 4). "Treason" means actually joining in a war against one's country and/or personally helping its enemies. This definition clarifies that criticizing the United States, its government or laws is not treason, but is protected as freedom of speech. Furthermore, a very high standard is set for proof:

> No Person shall be convicted of Treason unless on the Testimony of two Witnesses to the same overt Act, or on Confession in open Court.

"No Person" applies to everyone, both to common citizens and government officials. The act of treason has to be very obvious ("overt"), and two people have to see it. The only exception is if someone openly admits to committing treason, but such a confession must be "in open Court" – a confession in any other context is not sufficient. People are protected from being falsely accused of betraying the country and from being manipulated into a confession outside of court.

In the final clause, Congress is empowered to define the penalty for treason, setting official standards for the courts. (Under current law, this can be the death penalty, or alternatively a minimum of five years in prison plus a fine of at least $10,000.) Moreover, "attainder" is prohibited (see under Article I, Section 9, Clause 3), and punishment is limited to people who actually betray their country. Their property can be taken as long as they are alive, but their relatives do not lose their right to inherit. So-called "Corruption of Blood," the older idea in English law that kept people from claiming any inheritance from someone whose blood was deemed "corrupted," is explicitly banned.

Finally, like the president's assumed power to issue executive orders, one of the Supreme Court's most important powers is not specifically mentioned in the Constitution either. The Supreme Court maintains that it has the power of *"judicial review,"* i.e., the right to review objections to laws passed by Congress, and to even declare laws unconstitutional (see under Article VI). This means that the Supreme Court has the final say on many controversial issues, as it decides how to apply the Constitution to laws passed by states or by Congress. The nine justices hold an extremely powerful position, and as they often have different opinions and may split 5-4, one justice's vote one way or the other can dramatically impact how courts throughout the country are required to interpret the law.

5. American Federalism (Articles IV-VII)

After laying out the basic plan for the three branches of the government, the Constitution continues with four relatively short articles. In particular, these describe the American version of *federalism*, the concept of there being *both* a federal government for the whole republic and separate governments responsible for each state. As the relationship between these two levels must be clarified, the remaining articles address the status of the states (Article IV), the hierarchy of laws (Article VI), how this Constitution can be made official or "ratified" (Article VII), as well as how it can be amended (Article V).

The States (Article IV)

Article IV addresses Congress' powers over the states, focusing on their citizens' rights. Its contents parallel Article 4 of the Articles of Confederation, where the first sentence is taken from:

> Full Faith and Credit shall be given in each State to the public Acts, Records, and judicial Proceedings of every other State.

The phrase "Full Faith and Credit" indicates that states are expected to trust and acknowledge records from other states. Just as under the Confederation, all sorts of legal documents would continue to be recognized throughout the union, e.g., marriages, business contracts, wills, property, etc. Americans can neither lose rights nor escape obligations by going to a different state. Congress is here empowered to make laws ensuring that states honor this clause. However, the requirement of "full faith and credit" does not force states to accept other states' laws that *conflict* with their own laws. For example, some citizens may have a right to carry a weapon openly in their home state, but that does not mean that they keep this right in every state they enter. A more controversial example is same-sex marriage, which has been supported by some states but not by others. Should states (or the federal government) be required to recognize same-sex marriages from other states? Or do same-sex couples have to respect the laws of their state if it does not recognize this kind of union in exactly the same way as a traditional "marriage"? Until recently, the Supreme Court had largely confirmed the latter, leaving the issue up to the states. On the other hand, it had also allowed the courts to strike down a same-sex marriage ban in California and ruled that the federal government has to give benefits to same sex couples if their own state considers them married. In 2015, the Supreme Court finally went a step further and decided that same-sex couples who have been legally married in one state have to be treated equally under the marriage laws of other states as well (cf. the "equal protection" clause of Amendment XIV).

Section 2 continues by promising all American citizens the same "Privileges and Immunities," meaning that states have to give Americans from other states the same rights as their own citizens. On the other hand, states cannot offer them any special protection either. The second clause requires states to deliver people accused of crimes to each other if they flee from one state's justice system. The fact that this applies to any "Person," whether a citizen or not, sets the stage for the problematic third clause, which requires states to return any "Person held to Service or Labour" (i.e., a slave) who escapes and flees to another state. This meant that free states had to respect that slaves were "property" according to other states' laws, and had to return slaves who had escaped. This concession to slave owners was finally rendered void once slavery was abolished by Amendment XIII.

After the first two sections have clarified that states need to respect each other's laws, Section 3 moves on to give Congress authority to add new states and to make laws concerning territory under the government's control. The wording of being "admitted" to the United States implies that a potential state first requests to become a state, and Congress can then decide whether or not to admit it. This has happened numerous times, as the republic has grown from the original thirteen states to include fifty states since Alaska and Hawaii were admitted in 1959. Throughout its history, the United States has also possessed territories under its control, and most portions of these have ended up being admitted as states. It is possible that more states will be added from territories, for example Puerto Rico. Again, all that the Constitution demands is for the Senate and the House to accept a new state; there are no other formal requirements. Once admitted, then a state has all the same rights, protections, and duties as other states.

Section 3 mentions the possibility of new states forming from parts of existing states, which Congress can only permit if all the states involved approve. This has actually happened a few times when state legislatures have approved of part of their state leaving. The states of Maine, Kentucky and West Virginia broke away from other states, and Vermont was formed from areas claimed by two other states. The Constitution does not say anything, however, about states being able to leave the country once they are a part of it. As Congress is not specifically given this power, apparently it is not legally possible. When several states attempted to leave the union and declare themselves independent, this was not recognized by the federal government and led to the American Civil War (1861-1865). The southern states insisted that being part of the United States and accepting the Constitution was a free choice, and that they could leave the union. The North, on the other hand, insisted that states had no right to ever become independent again once they had joined the United States. The union victory in 1865 finally settled the issue in the latter's favor.

Article IV closes with Section 4, which specifies the duties the federal government has towards the states. First of all, it must "guarantee to every State in this Union a Republican form of Government." If a state's government is not based on fair representation, then the federal government must step in to protect the people's right to democratic participation. Secondly, states are promised military protection. If another country invades any state, the federal government has a constitutional obligation to use its military to protect and defend that state. Thirdly, the federal government has to help states bring internal conflicts ("domestic Violence") under control if they request it.

State governments tend to parallel the federal government's structure rather closely. They have their own state constitutions specifying citizens' rights and how laws are made and enforced in their state. Like the federal model, states have three branches of government. The people elect a state legislative branch, which has two chambers in every state except Nebraska, and a governor to head the executive branch. Each state has its own court system as well, also with a three-level structure including a state supreme court. The great majority of laws and court decisions in the United States are made at the state level. State laws can differ significantly from each other. Today, tax and business laws, gun laws, the death penalty, family law, abortion, marijuana, and physician-assisted suicide are just some of the issues that may be dealt with differently once one crosses over state lines.

Amending the Constitution (Article V)

Now that the new government's structure has been described, Article V explains how it can be modified in the future. It lays out two steps to amend the Constitution, namely, *proposing* and *ratifying*. An amendment can be *proposed* either by Congress or by a "Convention for proposing Amendments." Congress has to call a convention when two thirds of the states' legislatures officially request it. The details are not specified, and to date this has never actually been done. Nevertheless, the possibility of having to call a convention can influence Congress to propose an amendment itself before this happens. Congress needs a super-majority of two thirds, both in the House of Representatives and in the Senate separately. A proposed amendment only becomes "valid" once it is officially accepted or *ratified* by three-fourths of the states. Congress decides whether to leave ratification of an amendment up to state legislatures or to special state conventions. To date, the latter have ratified only one amendment (XXI), while otherwise state legislatures have always been responsible.

A couple things that Article V does *not* say are also significant. It does not say anything requiring states to take a position at all on proposed amendments; states can simply ignore them. As long as more than one fourth of the states have either rejected or have simply not dealt with an amendment, it cannot become part of the Constitution. Moreover, Article V does not put any time limits on proposed amendments. There are "open" amendments passed by Congress long ago, some as far back as 1810 or even 1789, which could still theoretically be ratified today if enough states chose to (see appendix). Once an amendment is proposed by two thirds of the House and of the Senate, it will simply wait to be ratified for however long that might take. On the other hand, it is possible to add a time limit for a particular amendment to be ratified, as the Constitution does not say anything *against* doing this.

Without the second step of ratification, proposed amendments have no binding legal authority. This two-step process and the demand for large majorities – two thirds in Congress and three fourths of the states – protects the Constitution from being altered without overwhelming support. It is thus not surprising that only 17 amendments have been added in the past 220 years. When they are passed, this often happens in clusters. Amendments XIII-XV were all ratified within a five-year period (1865-1870), then four amendments were added between 1913 and 1920. In 1933 two amendments were ratified, and yet another four between 1961 and 1971. Only two amendments (XXII, XXVII) were separated by more than six years from another amendment.

In contrast to the Articles of Confederation (Article 13), it is not necessary for *all* the states to ratify an amendment. Otherwise, even one single state could prevent an amendment from being added that the great majority of the country considers important. Finally, two restrictions are put on what kinds of amendments can be made. Two clauses in Article I, Section 9 are protected from being amended before the year 1808. Before that date, no amendment could empower the federal government to stop the slave trade (Clause 1) or to place a direct tax not based on population (Clause 4). In fact, each of these clauses was nullified respectively by Amendments XIII and XVI much later.

Constitutional Supremacy (Article VI)

Article VI seeks to clear up some final questions before closing. For one thing, adopting the Constitution does not invalidate obligations that the United States had while under the Articles of Confederation. In particular, the government was having serious difficulties paying France back for the large amounts of money it had loaned the United States during the Revolutionary War. Here it was made clear that adopting a new constitution would not be a way of trying to avoid this debt. Nor would diplomatic relations established with Europe be suddenly changed. The Constitution was to be an internal matter for the United States that would not create new tensions with other countries. After all, it would be controversial enough within the states.

The second paragraph of Article VI is known as the "supremacy clause" due to the statement calling the Constitution – as well as federal laws permitted by it ("in Pursuance thereof") and treaties – "the supreme Law of the land." Moreover, "the Judges in every State" are required to regard federal law as supreme, placing it above any conflicting law made by a state. The point here is to secure national order and ensure that the Constitution and laws passed by

Congress are really binding, so that states cannot simply disregard them. This principle is reflected in Article I, Section 10 as well, which limits states from assuming powers equal to or above what Congress can do.

Nevertheless, sometimes states do in fact ignore federal laws. They then hope that the administration has higher priorities than putting a lot of effort into trying to stop a state from doing what its people want. For example, marijuana is an illegal substance under federal law, but some states allow it for medical or even recreational purposes, thus technically violating the supremacy clause. In 2012, the state of Washington and Colorado completely legalized cannabis, and since then Alaska and Oregon have followed. Although the federal government sometimes insists on applying marijuana prohibitions against conflicting state laws, on the whole, it seems that this is not really enforceable. Since early 2015, personal possession of marijuana has even been legal in Washington, D.C., which the government has not stopped.

It is often debatable to what extent states can officially comply with federal laws at a minimum level while still enforcing their own laws. For example, while abortions are legal throughout the country under federal law, states can put limitations on them, for example by requiring them to be performed before the third trimester and by ensuring that the woman in question is presented with other options. Recently, in Texas strict requirements have dramatically limited the number of clinics where abortions can be performed. Technically, women still have a right to get an abortion in Texas, but critics argue that many women, especially in poorer areas, do not have equal and easy access to use this right.

The Supreme Court assumes the right to review and overrule any laws that – in its opinion – contradict the Constitution, or state laws that conflict with federal laws. This concept, known as "judicial review," goes back to the case *Marbury v. Madison* in 1803, when an act of Congress was declared to be unconstitutional. Congress had given the Supreme Court the right to issue orders to the executive branch, but the Court decided that its own jurisdiction is limited to the directives in Article III. Ironically, by rejecting an expansion of its power, the Supreme Court in fact asserted a great deal of authority! It established a precedent that it can decide whether laws are in keeping with the Constitution or not. This power is considered to be *implied* in Article III, Section 2, which gives the federal courts power to decide "all Cases …arising under this Constitution." Furthermore, it seems that the supremacy clause is not really enforceable unless judicial review is possible. Without it, there would be no way to stop Congress from passing laws that contradict the Constitution, "the supreme Law of the Land." After all, federal laws should only be treated as authoritative if they are "in Pursuance" of the Constitution, i.e., in agreement with it. Judicial review allows the federal courts to serve as a check on Congress and ensure that the proper hierarchy is respected – first the Constitution, then federal laws, and lastly state laws.

In keeping with this clear legal structure, all federal and state government officers of all branches (legislative, executive, judicial) are required to support the Constitution. They have to formally express this support by officially swearing an oath, which is traditionally done on the Bible. Alternatively, instead of an oath they can simply give an "Affirmation." This is essentially the same thing but does not have a religious connotation, thus guarding against excluding people from office on religious grounds. This was intended especially for Quakers, who consider "oaths" to go against Jesus' teaching (Matthew 5:37); three of the framers themselves were from Quaker families. In a modern context, the option of making an "affirmation" can also be used by nonreligious people. Sensitivity to a plurality of religious beliefs is expressed further in the statement that "no religious Test shall ever be required" for political office, including *any* position of responsibility for the people ("public Trust"). The emphatic word "ever" keeps this line against being amended at any time in the future. This restriction on religious tests is one of only two statements in the Constitution explicitly protected from ever being changed, the other being each state's equal representation in the Senate (Article V).

Keeping religious tests from excluding people who did not profess a certain set of beliefs must have been a serious personal concern for those who drafted and signed the Constitution. While a large number of them were affiliated with the Episcopal Church (the American version of the Church of England), other framers belonged to another Protestant church or none at all. Two were Roman Catholics, and probably feared that the overwhelmingly Protestant country might restrict certain offices to Protestants. Furthermore, some prominent framers, though professing belief in God and admiring Jesus' moral teachings, were skeptical of strict religious dogma and hardly wanted to be subjected to a test of traditional Christian orthodoxy.

While the requirement of an "Oath or Affirmation" is specifically applied to state offices as well, this ban on any "religious Test" appears to be specifically directed only to *federal* offices ("under the United States"). In fact, several states continued to demand their own political leaders to hold specific religious beliefs, and even today some states officially require their own government's officers to believe in God or a Supreme Being. However, if a state were to actually deny someone political office on purely religious grounds (something not likely to happen), the federal courts would presumably find a way to rule this unconstitutional.

Ratification (Article VII)

The final article emphasizes the agreement between the delegates from different states by referring to the "Unanimous Consent of the States Present." The phrase "Unanimous Consent" means that all parties were in agreement. The word "Present," however, betrays a problematic fact. If we look carefully at the states listed, we notice that there are only twelve – Rhode Island did not send any delegates, choosing not to take part. Furthermore, speaking of the "Consent of the *States*" gets around the fact that one delegate from Massachusetts and two from Virginia who were present refused to sign the Constitution. The five delegates from Virginia, the most populous state, were split almost in half, with George Washington's support breaking the tie. Even though there was not quite a unanimous consent of all the states or all the delegates, it was thus still possible to proclaim a "Unanimous Consent of the States Present." The fact that some delegates did not come at all precisely because they did not agree with the Constitution did not help their cause, but made it easier to proclaim the "Unanimous Consent" of those *present*! Only one of the delegates from New York, Alexander Hamilton, supported the Constitution. However, since the other New York delegates left the Convention early in disagreement with its nationalistic orientation, New York was counted in favor of the document based on Hamilton's vote alone.

The delegates' signatures serve as a "Witness" confirming that the Constitution was agreed upon, the final version being confirmed on September 17, 1787. It was not simply framed in the interest of one or two states, but by a general agreement between leaders from the several states. Nevertheless, many Americans, including delegates to the Convention and signers of the Declaration of Independence, objected, fearing that the Constitution gave too much power to Congress and lacked clear guarantees of the people's rights. In order to gain support for the Constitution in the face of this serious criticism, it was necessary to promise that a bill of rights would be added immediately to it in accord with Article V, which was in fact done.

Article VII also makes it clear that the Constitution will become binding once it is officially accepted, or "ratified," by nine states. These do so by forming conventions, which are to be made up of "Delegates, chosen in each State by the People." The state legislatures were expected to propose candidates and then let the people vote for them. There are no further instructions for these elections or conventions, nor is there any time limit. By leaving states free to organize the details for themselves and have their own elected delegates consider the Constitution, a positive response was made likely. In addition, as the common people, who were more afraid of having a central government than the upper classes were, could not vote directly on the Constitution, they would not be able to block the document from being passed. The framers thought it would be safer to leave the decision up to delegates, who were supposed to be more level-headed and better informed than the masses.

Finally, Article VII declares that as soon as nine states accept the Constitution, it will be binding for them ("between the States so ratifying the same"), but not for any other states. The explanation after the signatures made clear that Congress would immediately start acting under the directions of the new Constitution once this minimum of nine ratifications had been reached. It would then set dates for electing the president and the new Congress of senators and representatives so that the new government could take its place. When the United States began operating under the Constitution on March 4, 1789, eleven states had accepted it, not including North Carolina and Rhode Island. As the country began moving forward without these two states and put them under pressure to join them, they finally accepted the Constitution as well, though independently-minded Rhode Island did not give in until over a year later. Since then, the United States has operated under the basic framework of this Constitution up to the present day.

6. Basic Liberties of Citizens (Amendments I-IV)

When the Constitution was first proposed, many Americans feared that the new government could become tyrannical unless specific rights were guaranteed to citizens. The British had a Bill of Rights limiting the monarch's powers, and after declaring independence, the states started making such lists of their own to protect their citizens from their respective state governments. Although the framers generally defended the Constitution's system of checks and balances as sufficient to limit governmental power, many Americans were hesitant to accept the document unless more explicit protection of citizens' rights was added. Several states officially requested this, and critics pointed to the lack of a list of rights to gain support for voting against the Constitution. James Madison, who had initially insisted that a national bill of rights was unnecessary, was finally persuaded not only to support one, but even to write it himself! Using his own state of Virginia's Declaration of Rights as a model, Madison brought twelve *articles of amendment* before the first Congress under the Constitution in 1789, which were all approved. Two of these were forgotten without being ratified (but see under Amendment XXVII). The remaining ten, which specifically protected citizens' rights, were quickly ratified by 1791 in accordance with Article V. To this day, the *Bill of Rights* is highly regarded in the United States as guaranteeing the people's rights and freedoms. It is seen as a fundamental part of the American tradition and national identity. The first four of these ten amendments, which are discussed in this chapter, establish basic *liberties* citizens have concerning *religion* and *expression* (I) as well as *security* (II-IV).

Freedom of Religion (Amendment I, Clause 1)

The First Amendment includes some of the best known statements in the entire Constitution. The first clause addresses *religion* in two sub-clauses known as (a) the *establishment clause* and (b) the *free exercise clause*, which read as follows:

> (a) Congress shall make no law respecting an establishment of religion
> (b) or prohibiting the free exercise thereof

In keeping with the establishment clause, the federal government has never demanded a church tax or given unique privileges to a particular church. Many religious communities in the United States had faced persecution in Europe, and had even immigrated for this reason. Based on these negative experiences, many Americans feared that a national church would limit the religious freedom and equality of those who worshipped in a different manner. Such concerns had also motivated prohibiting religious tests for public office in Article VI.

Originally, however, the First Amendment did not necessarily restrict having an "establishment of religion" at the *state* level. The First Amendment even begins with *"Congress* shall make no law…" – *not* "the states shall make no law." While a *national* church was ruled out, some of the founders (e.g., John Adams, George Washington) still supported having an official church in their own state. In the decades that followed, more Americans increasingly found an official link between church and government problematic even at the state level. Members of minority churches and others were put at a disadvantage, and state governments became entangled in church affairs. One by one, the states themselves disestablished their own churches, the last one being Massachusetts in 1833. States often still continued to express support for religion in general, but not for one specific church.

Even with regard to the federal government, the First Amendment has never banned prayers and language about God in public life. This general *"civil" religion* is not connected with any church, and the official motto of the United States, "In God We Trust," is open for

Americans to interpret in their own way. Thanksgiving Day is celebrated as a day for all Americans (of all religious beliefs) to thank the Creator. When Congress opens meetings with a prayer or when the president asks for God's blessings over the country, such actions are generally not seen as violating the establishment clause, as they do not promote any specific church. An "establishment of religion" has historically been understood as a *particular* religion, a completely separate issue from a *general* belief in a Creator. In many European countries the exact opposite is the case. References to "God" are rare in public politics, but churches are officially privileged by the state. One way of putting it is that the United States has a very strict separation between *church* and state (stricter than in many European countries), but no separation at all between *God* and state. As there has always been a variety of religious groups in United States, even at the start there was a clear distinction between God and the various churches that worship according to their own rules and beliefs.

From the start, most Americans have professed some form of Christianity. As the country has grown more religiously diverse, however, Christian symbols on *public property* and religious content in *public schools* have become very controversial. Since the 1940s, the courts have interpreted the establishment clause more broadly, sometimes even seeing various Christian groups as together forming an unofficial religious "establishment." Due to its cultural significance, Christmas Day is a national holiday. As state "Christmas trees," however, are criticized for allegedly promoting Christianity on state property, state governments often choose the legal fiction of decorating a "*holiday* tree." A particularly controversial issue has been displaying the Ten Commandments at court houses, a central question here being to what extent such displays actually further the Christian religion or simply celebrate the nation's cultural heritage.

Historically, generically Christian (i.e., Protestant) prayer and Bible reading were often allowed in public schools as long as they were not linked with one particular church. Starting in the 1960s, however, the Supreme Court has restricted such activities as violating a *broad* interpretation of the establishment clause. Today, teachers in public schools can no longer lead prayers in class, and have to teach evolution. School prayer can too easily promote quite specific religious ideas, and creationism (the teaching that God created the world in six days, not by evolution) is based on a specific, literal interpretation of the Bible. The question of whether teaching "intelligent design," a more general theory of special creation (without reference to the Bible), should be permitted in public schools alongside evolution, remains controversial. Furthermore, American children receive religious instruction at their own places of worship, often in the form of "Sunday school," but not at all in public schools.

The *free exercise clause* guarantees the freedom to believe and worship according to one's conscience. In the founding period, many Protestants were afraid of other Protestant churches (!) treating them in an unequal way. The Roman Catholic minority (including two signers of the Constitution), not having been given equal rights in England, was of course concerned about religious liberty in a Protestant society. Nevertheless, some groups have been denied equal rights in the United States because they were not seen as legitimate "religions." In the past, Native American religions were often disregarded since they lack the kind of organization and structure typical of many religions, but today they are strongly protected as well.

As all religious beliefs are equally protected by the free exercise clause, the state must show a basic level of respect to all religious groups, no matter how small in number or extreme in their views. Unlike many countries, the United States government cannot warn against religious movements unless there is a *direct* threat of *violence* involved. The free exercise clause can also be the basis for religious groups to get exemptions from the law. From the start, members of religious communities with pacifist beliefs have been exempt from serving in the military. Today, Native Americans are allowed to use substances in religious ceremonies that are otherwise considered illegal drugs. Groups such as the Amish and the Jehovah's Witnesses have won a number of court cases ensuring that they do not have to follow rules conflicting with their particular religious beliefs. Moreover, Americans who do not want to send their children to secular, public schools for religious (or other) reasons can homeschool them. The free exercise clause also gives Muslim women and girls a solid legal basis for wearing headscarves in public schools and at work. (Full face coverings, however, are problematic due to identity and security concerns.) For many people in the world, the religious diversity in the United States and the open display of religion may seem shocking. For many Americans, the fact that all citizens may very openly express and promote their beliefs without any direction or restrictions from the government is considered one of their most fundamental rights.

As already indicated, a public "civil religion" is widespread in the United States. Most Americans still profess to be Christians, and there are many who emphasize the Christian heritage of their country. General references to "God" are thus often widely understood in a Christian sense, but the civil religion can also include other beliefs. The national song "God Bless America" was written by an American Jew, and may be sung by American Muslims. While the great majority of Americans say they believe in God (in one way or another), the rise of secularism and even atheism in recent decades has brought new challenges as to how to apply the First Amendment. Especially among the younger generation, the number of non-religious Americans is considerably on the rise. Still, American students see the national motto "In God We Trust" and salute the flag while saying they are part of "One nation under God." This kind of language is generally accepted, as it is part of the national tradition and is open to interpretation. Atheists, who also have a right to equal protection, may openly object to such statements, and their children are exempt from making them in public schools. Atheists often argue, however, that state support of an undefined "God" unfairly excludes them and violates a very broad understanding of the establishment clause. On the other hand, most Americans feel that their right to free exercise includes publically acknowledging God or a Higher Power at official events, and that a minority of atheists should not be able to banish this national tradition. Moreover, although oaths (e.g., in court) are traditionally sworn on the Bible, people have the option of not using any book. In very rare cases other religious books may be used. Members of Congress are also usually sworn in on the Bible, though this is not required. In 2006, the first Muslim elected to the House of Representatives was sworn in on the Quran.

A current controversy about religious freedom has arisen with the legalization of same-sex marriage. Can business owners who do not believe in same-sex "marriage" on religious grounds deny wedding-related services to gay and lesbian couples? Or are businesses required to, for example, bake cakes or provide flowers to any customers who request them? The Religious Freedom Restoration Act passed by the state of Indiana in 2015 drew considerable criticism, as it could possibly be used to legally protect people who do not feel comfortable with their business supporting same-sex weddings. The actual long-term effects of this law, or other similar laws in other states, have yet to be seen. Moreover, there are still many open questions about educational institutions and social charity organizations sponsored by religious groups that do not accept same-sex marriage. Are they allowed, for instance, to only provide housing to traditional marriage couples? On the other hand, will the government be allowed to deny them tax exemptions if they discriminate against same-sex couples in any way? Such issues will likely be battled over in the courts, and may well need to be settled by a Supreme Court decision in the near future.

Freedom of Expression (Amendment I, Clause 2)

In addition to the issues of religious establishment and religious freedom, the First Amendment also prohibits laws

> ...abridging the freedom of speech, or of the press; or the right of the people peaceably to assemble, and to petition the Government for a redress of grievances.

These guarantees reflect a general right of *freedom of expression*. Citizens are allowed to freely say and print their opinions – even if the government does not like them. People can also come together to ask the government to set right something they believe it has done wrong ("redress of grievances"). Only peaceful gatherings, not ones that are violent, are protected. The rights of assembly and petition have generally been understood as one right – the people can gather *in order to* petition the government. (After all, the word "or" separates the other rights, while these two are joined together by "and.") The authorities are not allowed to stop people from criticizing the government or protesting. The freedom of expression helps keep the government accountable to its citizens and ensures people that they have nothing to fear if they speak their mind.

Freedom of expression applies especially to *opinions* concerning personal beliefs and criticism of the government's policies, but not necessarily in other contexts. Pornographic material was originally not protected at all by the First Amendment, but is permitted today (except for child pornography) as long as it is not especially "obscene," a term that may be interpreted differently by courts in different states and regions. Leaking secret government information is not protected as freedom of speech either, and can lead to be being prosecuted for betraying the United States. Directly provoking violence, threatening to attack somebody, copying other people's works, and willfully spreading lies about individuals or groups to damage their reputation are not protected either and may be punished in court.

However, if ideas expressed do not clearly fall into these kinds of categories, they are strongly protected. For example, publically denying the Holocaust – something that can be punished by fines and even prison sentences in many European countries today – is allowed in the United States with hardly any serious legal debate. Expressing racist opinions is also legal as long as it does not directly call for violence against anyone. In a controversial ruling, the Supreme Court has also decided that the First Amendment allows Americans to publically burn the nation's flag to express their opposition to the government.

In comparison to many countries, the United States may seem to have a relaxed attitude towards even the most questionable of opinions. Claims that hateful opinions could perhaps *indirectly* lead to violence are generally quickly dismissed, but any *direct* threat is another matter. If someone claims that a certain group of people is inferior or that the American government will soon be demolished by God, such is clearly permitted by law. The police will even protect people who want to publically promote such views. However, the moment someone calls for a specific *attack* or threatens *violence* against anyone, authorities take this very seriously. In particular, planning or threatening terrorist actions is obviously not protected as freedom of speech.

Traditionally, the freedom of the press is thought to protect a so-called "fourth estate," a sort of independent institution that can keep an additional check on the three branches of government. The press is supposed to be free to criticize the government and inform the people about abuses of power, thus making the government more careful about its actions. However, many are concerned that the relationship of the press to the government may have gotten too close, as the press regularly listens to government in suppressing information. The government insists that classified information that could harm the United States or make it difficult, for example, to successfully fight against terrorism, must be kept secret. Critics still contend, however, that there is a danger of the press acting too protectively of its government in support of the war on terror instead of reporting freely and critically.

Arms and the Security of a Free State (Amendment II)

Amendments II-IV deal with the people's *security* and with keeping governmental authorities from invading their private space. The Second Amendment emphasizes "security" in terms of a right to have weapons. As mentioned earlier (cf. under Article I, Section 8, Clause 14-15), militias are state military units and played a role in the American Revolution. The Articles of Confederation had stated:

> ... every State shall always keep up a well-regulated and disciplined militia, sufficiently armed and accoutered, and shall provide and constantly have ready for use, in public stores, a due number of filed pieces and tents, and a proper quantity of arms, ammunition and camp equipage. (Articles of Confederation VI, Clause 4)

This very recent background from the Revolutionary War was a living memory for many Americans. Organized, armed state militias were important for protecting the rebelling colonies from British forces, and it was thought they would continue to help keep people safe from invasions, as well as from Indian raids. If the new government under the Constitution had tried to limit militias or take the people's weapons away, this would certainly have been seen as a tyrannical act endangering the people and the freedoms they had fought for. Furthermore, it would have made the people entirely dependent on the government, leaving them helpless to continue defending themselves. In this historical context, it is not surprising that the Second Amendment guaranteed the following right:

> A well regulated Militia, being necessary to the security of a free State, the right of the people to keep and bear Arms, shall not be infringed.

This amendment is unique in that it gives a specific *reason* for the right to carry weapons – a "well regulated Militia" is needed. People have a right to carry weapons so that they, as groups of citizens, can protect their communities and states. Congress currently recognizes both an "organized" and an "unorganized" militia of the United States. The nationwide organized militia today takes the shape of the National Guard, which is made up of people who hold civilian jobs but are also in part-time military service. They are "on call" to support their state and the nation militarily when needed. In addition, many (but not all) states also maintain their very own state defense forces or state militias independent from the National Guard. Finally, the so-called unorganized militia has been identified by Congress as including all physically able men between the ages of 17 and 44, and former military members until age 64.

Both the National Guard and state militias outside the federal system are firmly protected by the Second Amendment. Many question, however, if the same can necessarily be said about gun ownership rights for a general "unorganized" militia; the Second Amendment speaks explicitly of a "well organized" one. Do *individuals* have a constitutional "right to bear arms" for private use or personal protection even without being directly related to a "well regulated Militia"? Recently, the Supreme Court has answered in the affirmative, arguing that states, cities, and districts cannot restrict their people's individual right to own and have reasonable access to personal weapons. It has argued that a right given to "the people" must also be applied to individuals, as elsewhere in the Bill of Rights. Earlier in American history, the "right to bear arms" was interpreted more closely in connection with militias, but today it is largely dealt with as a very *personal* issue. Like the First Amendment, the Second Amendment has also been given an increasingly broad interpretation.

Banning weapons altogether would obviously conflict with "the right of the people to bear arms." However, even if this is understood as a right applying to individuals, exactly what kind of weapons they can own and under what circumstances they can carry them can still differ significantly from state to state. Many (but not all) states have banned "assault weapons." In many states it is allowed to carry a weapon openly, even without a permit. In other states, people are required to first obtain a permit before they can buy a gun, and they are not allowed to carry weapons at all in public, even if hidden. Furthermore, even in the same state gun laws are typically stricter in cities than in the country.

The Second Amendment raises sensitive, emotional issues. For many Americans, restricting gun ownership would threaten a basic right and make them more dependent on the government. They want a "free State," not a police state. Other Americans believe that their own state or city should – in the interest of public safety – be able to regulate and even restrict weapons that are not connected with an organized militia. They are concerned that the federal government's interference in protecting individual gun ownership can hinder them from keeping their own states and communities safe in the ways that they think best.

A further question is *when* individuals are allowed to actually *use* the weapons they legally own. Most (but not all) states permit people to shoot anyone who breaks into their home. Many states go even beyond this rule, allowing citizens to use a weapon against anyone who attacks or threatens them *anywhere*, without requiring them to first try to escape. Such laws, known as "stand-your-ground" laws, are intended to provide legal protection for people who may need to defend themselves against criminals; they will not be considered guilty of a crime if they use a weapon against someone who first violently threatens them. Requiring people to try to get away could make them vulnerable to criminals who may attack or shoot them while they are doing so. On the other hand, there is a serious danger that stand-your-ground laws can lead to people being wrongly killed if they are *perceived* as threatening. In some cases, a struggle between two people can lead to one of them being killed, and the other one can claim to have been attacked first and to thus have full legal protection unless their version of the story can be *proven* wrong.

In recent years, the combination of lenient gun laws with racial prejudices has become increasingly central in the national debate about restrictions on weapons. In 2012, when Trayvon Martin, an unarmed black teenager, was shot on his way home by a neighborhood watch coordinator who said that Martin had acted suspiciously and aggressively, the concept of stand-your-ground laws was called into question nationwide. In 2015, after a racist shooter entered an historic black church and killed nine people, President Obama called for more discussion about how stricter gun regulations might help prevent such incidents. Many argue that easy access to weapons makes racist shootings easier and leads to disproportionate shootings of blacks. Others question, however, if stricter weapons regulations would really be effective, and if they could end up giving police another reason to search poor blacks suspected of having weapons. In any case, gun violence motivated by racism makes questions about gun law especially urgent.

Security and Privacy (Amendments III-IV)

The Third Amendment, in contrast to its predecessor, is not controversial. It protects people's right to their own property by prohibiting the military to force any citizen to house soldiers. There may be exceptions "in time of war," but only if Congress specifically makes a law defining the conditions (which it has not done). This amendment was particularly important at the time because the British had demanded American colonists to house their soldiers. Many Americans wanted to ensure that their government would never be able to do this. Beyond this situation, the Third Amendment also implies a general right to *privacy and private property* protected from the government and military.

This general concern is dealt with further in the Fourth Amendment. Echoing the Second Amendment, it again mentions *security* as well as a "right of the people." They have a right "to be secure in their persons, houses, papers and effects, against unreasonable searches and seizures." Government officials cannot simply search people or take anything from them ("effects" signify any personal items of property) without first justifying these actions as "reasonable." Ultimately, the courts decide whether specific "searches and seizures" are "unreasonable" or not. In order to search someone's home, the authorities need a *warrant*, a court order allowing them to do so. This forces the police to first convince a judge that they have good reason to believe ("probable cause") that someone has committed a particular crime. The warrant must be very specific, "describing the place to be searched, and the persons or things to be seized." If police break into a person's house without a warrant and obtain evidence, it cannot be used in court, because it was obtained illegally.

In the 21st century, the Fourth Amendment "right ...to be secure" has been re-interpreted in connection with national security and the so-called "war on terror." The "Patriot Act," passed by Congress shortly after the fateful terrorist attacks on September 11, 2001, permits wiretapping suspected terrorists on any phone line they use. It also empowers federal agencies to gather a wide range of private information on anyone considered *relevant* for investigations related to terrorism and to seize their property, even if the person in question is not accused of any crime. While intended to make it easier for the government to catch terrorists and protect the people, serious concerns have been raised about these surveillance activities, which go beyond those that have traditionally been permitted. Under the Patriot Act, searches have been conducted that ignore the Fourth Amendment's demand for a court to first agree that there is good reason ("probable cause") to suspect criminal activity. Some of the most blatant of such violations have been struck down by the federal courts.

In June 2013, the discussion about privacy rights and the government's duty to protect its people entered an even more serious stage. The issue was raised by Edward Snowden, a computer specialist working for the National Security Agency (NSA), which operates as part of the Department of Defence, one of the fifteen departments in the government's executive branch. Snowden revealed to the public that the NSA has easy access to people's private phone records and internet searches as well as to their email and social network activity. Such actions, Snowden contended, disregard the Fourth Amendment's protection against "unreasonable searches" without a warrant.

In response, President Obama has insisted that monitoring suspicious private messages online and looking through phone records can help the government to find terrorists. Furthermore, the president has argued that the constitutional system of *checks and balances* keeps the NSA from abusing its access to people's personal data. The surveillance activities are being overseen by members of Congress who help keep the executive branch in check, and if any citizens are harmed by having their rights violated, they will be able to challenge the government in court. From the government's perspective, its surveillance powers to find terrorists are central to its constitutional responsibility to "provide for the common Defence and general Welfare of the United States," as well as "To make all Laws which shall be necessary and proper" to this end (Article I, Section 8).

Whether the government's expanded ability to conduct "searches and seizures" is "unreasonable" or not (Amendment IV), and whether this is truly "necessary and proper," are issues currently being debated in the United States. If the people disagree with the way Congress applies these requirements (or fails to), they have the possibility to write their representatives and senators and even to protest in the hope of changing their minds (Amendment I). If they find it necessary, the people can then elect new officials who will be able to change the laws to correspond more closely to their own understanding of their constitutional rights. To what extent are American voters prepared to give up certain aspects of privacy in exchange for the promise of greater protection? With the threat of terrorism on the one hand and of an intrusive government on the other hand, Americans are being faced with some difficult questions regarding how to balance liberty and security.

These issues are complicated by the Internet, where "private" messages are sent on a "public" server. Should people's activity online be protected just as documents or conversations in their homes would be, or at least like private telephone conversations or letters, or does the World Wide Web count as a *public* sphere not subject to the same privacy standards? Finally, while in the United States discussions about privacy rights focus on *American citizens*, the *international* community has become very concerned as well. Foreign nationals cannot necessarily claim any rights under the Constitution of the United States. Although they cannot be prosecuted by the American government either, many citizens of other countries still demand a right to privacy and are disturbed by the idea of foreign government workers being able to spy on them and read their private messages. The American government, on the other hand, justifies internet surveillance as part of its duty to protect its own people against potential foreign attacks.

7. Rights Under the Justice System (Amendments V-X)

After promising liberties regarding religion, expression, security and privacy, the Bill of Rights continues by protecting citizens accused of breaking the law (Amendments V, VI, VII). Before the state is allowed to punish anyone, it first has to prove that the person is guilty in the context of *"due process of law,"* i.e., a fair legal procedure (Amendment V). One important aspect is the role of *juries*, groups of citizens that decide whether the accused should be brought to court (V), whether a person has been proven guilty in a trial (VI), or who is right when two citizens have a dispute with each other (VII). This institution, inherited from England, is based on the principle that people should be judged by impartial, randomly selected fellow citizens. The state cannot bring a citizen to trial or convict them of a crime without the people's approval. Amendment VIII goes on to make sure that even those who are imprisoned and found guilty still have some basic legal protection. Finally, as an "appendix" to the Bill of Rights, Amendments IX and X provide for further issues and rights that are not specifically addressed in the Constitution.

Basic Rights of the Accused (Amendment V)

The Fifth Amendment mentions the right to a "Grand Jury," which decides whether or not a citizen should be "indicted," i.e., officially accused of a crime and brought to trial. This right is limited to cases involving "a capital, or otherwise infamous crime," meaning serious criminal charges. This grand jury, which comes from the older English system, no longer exists in England, but still lives on in the United States. The point is that a citizen should not be forced to go to court at all unless fellow citizens agree that this is reasonable. The state has to present its evidence before a randomly chosen group of 16 to 25 citizens, and only if a majority agrees is it allowed to take the accused person to court. Today, while all Americans have a fundamental right to a grand jury in *federal* cases, whether or not this is practiced on the state level depends on the state. Furthermore, the Fifth Amendment makes exceptions even for federal cases dealing with the military, and also for cases in the militia "when in actual service in time of War or public Danger." A trial can be started more quickly and easily in military contexts.

Recently, major concerns have been raised about the grand jury requirement, especially when racial aspects are involved. In two separate high-profile cases in 2014, white police officers who killed black suspects during attempted arrests were not indicted by the grand jury, and so avoided ever being brought to trial. One of them had shot Michael Brown, a young unarmed black man, in Ferguson, Missouri, where protests soon gained international attention. Frustration was fuelled by the situation of a mostly black community having a predominantly white police force. The other incident was the killing of Eric Garner, a black man in poor health who died after being held to the ground by a police officer. In both of these cases, many felt that the police officers were unfairly protected from legal prosecution.

Besides the grand jury, the Fifth Amendment guarantees additional rights. No one can "be subject for the same offence to be twice put in jeopardy of life or limb." The latter phrase "jeopardy [i.e., danger] of life or limb" is broadly interpreted to include criminal charges with serious penalties. Known as the *double jeopardy* clause, this means that nobody can be tried for the same crime twice by the same authority. If someone is declared innocent by a jury, then the state cannot try that person ever again for that crime, even if new evidence appears. This principle gives the state only *one chance* to convict someone and gives citizens the security that a case against them is really over for good. On the other hand, the double jeopardy clause does not necessarily rule out someone being tried once by *state* authorities and another time by a *federal* court or even in a *civil* court by a fellow citizen. Moving on, the next clause states that no one "shall be compelled in any criminal case to be a witness against himself." People cannot be forced to answer questions or say anything that could make them appear guilty. This Fifth Amendment right, generally understood as a right to *silence*, is affirmed when American police tell people who are arrested: "You have the right to remain silent. Anything you say can and will be used against you in a court of law."

The Fifth Amendment continues with the *due process* clause, which might reasonably be seen as the heart of the Bill of Rights. According to this central constitutional guarantee, nobody can "be deprived of life, liberty, or property, without due process of law." Amendments I-IV define "liberty" and assume "property" rights, while Amendments V-VIII set forth the guidelines for "due process." If the accused is denied a jury, a fair trial, etc. (see also under Amendments VI-VII), then the federal government is not permitted to take away their "life, liberty, or property." Later, Amendment XIV re-affirmed the due process clause, explicitly applying it to the *state* governments as well.

While primarily protecting people from being unjustly punished, the due process clause is also relevant for the current debate about *privacy* rights (see under Amendment IV). Are citizens deprived of "liberty" without legitimate "due process" when government workers review their private phone records and monitor their online activity? Or are such actions permissible as long as the government stays within the bounds of the powers given by Congress and does not limit freedom of speech?

One controversial issue concerning due process today is the government's use of unmanned aircrafts known as *drones* to target and kill terrorist leaders. The current administration has justified such actions if someone's terrorist involvement is clearly demonstrated (by secret, classified information), and if it is difficult to arrest them (i.e., because they are hiding in a foreign country). That is, anyone, even an American citizen, who is planning attacks on the United States is dealt with by standards used in wartime. The

Fifth Amendment's exception to requiring indictment by a grand jury in cases of "public danger" might be seen as permitting the government to go around the normal standards of due process in cases that pose an imminent threat to the American people.

Critics, however, protest that the government taking away "life" without giving suspects any kind of trial clearly violates the right to "due process" and sets a dangerous precedent. Many are particularly concerned by the fact that drones have even been used against American citizens, and have accidently killed other Americans who were not accused of any crime. Furthermore, as the evidence used to justify drone strikes is not open to the public, it seems the government could theoretically kill just about anyone and claim they were a terrorist, whether or not there is really evidence that would stand up in court. The government does not have to indict the accused or demonstrate their guilt in a public trial. The administration, on the other hand, insists that it only authorizes strikes in order to protect Americans in what are essentially war-like circumstances. As long as these actions are allowed by Congress under certain conditions, involving a careful (private) review process of the evidence, then the government insists that "due process" has been respected, at least as understood under modern anti-terror laws.

The Fifth Amendment's final clause does not deal with situations involving criminal charges, but reads: "nor shall private property be taken for public use without just compensation." This "takings clause" might seem out of place in the Bill of Rights since it gives the government a power not even mentioned elsewhere in the Constitution. Apparently, it was assumed that it would sometimes be necessary for the government to take and use private property, and here owners are given some protection since they have to at least receive "just compensation." While some actions such as taking property needed for public roads are generally accepted, the Supreme Court has recently interpreted the phrase "public use" very broadly, allowing the government to take property and sell it to private developers planning to use it in a way that will *benefit* the public (e.g., creating jobs, and making the community more attractive). As this interpretation seems to essentially let the government take property from one private individual and give it to another, it has been widely criticized. Even in this case, the Fifth Amendment at least still guarantees that the person whose property is taken will be given a fair market price in return.

Further Rights of the Accused (Amendments VI-VII)

The Fifth Amendment's requirement of "due process of law" is defined further in the Sixth Amendment, which addresses "all criminal proceedings" once a person has been indicted. While the previous amendment mentioned the "grand jury," the kind of jury meant here actually listens to the trial and decides whether the accused person is guilty or not. This "trial jury" or "petit jury" (i.e., "little jury") is typically composed of twelve members. This right was already mentioned in Article III, Section 2, Clause 3. Here, the word "impartial" is added, which has for example been used to demand sufficient racial diversity on juries so that they are not overly biased. Moreover, while Article III implies that the jury has to be from the same state as the crime, Amendment VI adds specifically that it even needs to be from the same district, a smaller region in the state already specified before the crime occurred. Not removed outsiders, but people from the same general community affected are responsible for passing judgment. As with the grand jury, Americans do not necessarily have a right to a trial by jury for minor offences (e.g., parking violations) with a relatively light penalty, but only for serious criminal charges.

The Sixth Amendment guarantees "the right to a speedy and public trial." Any defendant (a citizen accused of a crime) can demand the trial to take place reasonably soon, in order to not have to wait indefinitely to be cleared of charges. People typically agree to give this right up, since it may often be more difficult to be proven guilty if more time has passed since the crime was committed. The right to a *public* trial ensures that the process is not conducted in secret, so that the state remains accountable to the people (this right can, however, be limited if in the interest of the defendant). In reality, most cases are not decided by public jury trials, but by so-called *plea bargaining*. Most Americans accused of crimes choose not to use their rights under the Sixth Amendment, but instead confess to the crime and plead "guilty" in exchange for being given a lesser punishment than they would receive if convicted by a jury.

Nevertheless, a defendant has the right to insist on a trial. Besides the rights to a "speedy and public trial" decided "by an impartial jury" from the district of the crime, the accused also has the right (a) to be told the details ("the nature and cause") of the charges in advance, (b) "to be confronted with the witnesses," being able to question and challenge them, (c) to request favorable witnesses who have to testify in court ("compulsory process"), and (d) "to have the assistance of counsel," i.e., a lawyer to defend them. The courts, then, have a duty to ensure that defendants can make use of these rights if they demand them. At a defendant's request, a court can force witnesses to come before it (whether they want to speak or not). In current practice, the court even has to provide a defense lawyer if the defendant cannot afford one. This right and the Fifth Amendment right to silence are together known as the "Miranda rights" since they were confirmed by the Supreme Court in the landmark case *Miranda v. Arizona* in 1966.

While the Fifth and Sixth Amendments deal with *criminal* cases, in which the *state* accuses someone of a crime, the Seventh Amendment addresses *civil* cases ("Suits at common law"). These are cases in which one citizen accuses another in court. In such disputes, there is also a "right of trial by jury" as long as the minimum requirement of "twenty dollars" is at stake. (This amount is worth much less today than it was in the 18th century.) As it is often considered too expensive and time-consuming for state courts to have to select a jury for almost *every* dispute between citizens, this right is only seen as binding on the *federal* court system, which is specifically mentioned in this context ("any Court of the United States"). Once a jury has decided a civil law suit, this can only be "re-examined" by a federal court if it applies the standards of the "common law" system (the traditional principles used in the legal system inherited from England). According to those rules, the judge cannot actually reverse the decision made by a jury, but can demand a re-trial if a serious error was made in the trial process.

Rights of the Imprisoned and Convicted (Amendment VIII)

The Eighth Amendment guarantees at least some degree of rights to prisoners, including those who have been convicted of the most serious crimes. Specifically, it rules out (a) "Excessive bail," (b) "excessive fines," and (c) "cruel and unusual punishments." The first point applies to people in prison awaiting trial who may be released by a deposit, and the second point applies to people who have to pay a fine for breaking the law. In both cases, what is "excessive" may depend on the crime and the circumstances; the exact amount of money considered not unreasonably "excessive" is determined by the courts and by law. These specifications ensure that a person cannot be subjected to much higher bail or fines than other people in similar circumstances. Thirdly, regardless of what someone may have done, "cruel and unusual punishments" are here denounced, clearly outlawing all forms of torture. What is regarded as "unusual" depends on how common certain punishments are. Historically, making prisoners do hard labor was accepted, as this practice was widespread, at least in some areas of the country. Since the 1950s, however, prisoner "chain gangs" for labor have generally disappeared in the United States. In any case, Amendment VIII has always outlawed singling out certain prisoners and punishing them in ways that are "unusual" by the standards generally applied to prisoners. These standards, of course, may and do change with time.

In the modern legal debate, the question arises as to what extent the Eighth Amendment should apply to capital punishment, i.e., the *death penalty*. When the Bill of Rights was ratified, this was not an issue. The Fifth Amendment clearly implies that people can be deprived of "life" if convicted of murder after being given a fair trial and "due process of law." But should the death penalty today be ruled out today by a modern understanding of "cruel and usual"? The Eighth Amendment has been used to outlaw capital punishment for anything except for murder. Moreover, as forms of death that may cause great suffering are considered "cruel," lethal injection has become the standard form. In recent years, the Supreme Court has ruled that the Eighth Amendment does not allow giving the death penalty to the mentally disabled or to minors. Several states have outlawed the death penalty altogether, and many use it only in rare cases. However, as long as the majority of states do permit using it as a punishment for murder, it is not likely that the Supreme Court will consider it "unusual."

The rights of the accused and prisoners guaranteed in these amendments are applicable to American citizens, and to non-citizens in the country. They do not, however, necessarily apply to non-citizens in other parts of the world taken prisoner or accused of crimes by the United States. After World War II, war criminals in Germany were flatly denied a right to trial by jury. The fact that the American military had taken control did not mean that Germans suddenly gained all the rights of American citizens under the Constitution. The United States officially accepts international legal guidelines as formulated by the Geneva Conventions and of course does not, e.g., condone torture in any context. In recent years, as the treatment of "enemy combatants" has been subject to criticism, the United States has punished obvious breaches of international law that occurred in its military prisons. Holding war prisoners deemed to pose a terrorist threat in Guantanamo Bay remains controversial, both internationally and in the United States. The Supreme Court has given prisoners there a right to request American federal courts to review their cases, as Guantanamo Bay, although not actually part of the United States, is under American control.

Rights not Mentioned Here (Amendments IX-X)

One of the chief criticisms about adding a bill of rights was that it could be used to *limit* rights to those specifically mentioned. Since listing *all* rights seemed impossible, the Ninth Amendment ensures that "The enumeration in the Constitution of certain rights shall not be construed to deny or disparage others retained by the people." That is, the Bill of Rights can only be used to protect liberties and rights, *not* to suggest that citizens *only* have these rights and no others. In the English "common law" tradition, based on legal principles common to the whole country, precedents set by the courts are binding for the future. Rights traditionally assumed by the courts cannot suddenly be taken away. Today, the Ninth Amendment's main function is to strengthen rights that are *implied* elsewhere in the Bill of Right. For example, a basic "right to privacy" cannot be denied simply since these words are not *explicitly* stated in the Constitution. The Ninth Amendment helps ensure that this right assumed by Amendments III and IV is to be applied in a variety of contexts. It also helps keep "due process" from being limited to the requirements specifically described in the Bill of Rights. For example, special rules need to be considered if a mentally ill person or a minor is accused of a crime.

The Tenth Amendment is also meant to keep the federal government from expanding its authority. It reads:

> The powers not delegated to the United States by the Constitution, nor prohibited by it to the States, are reserved to the States respectively, or to the people.

The federal government is only permitted to take actions it can justify by the Constitution. If the Constitution does not (a) give it a power or (b) prohibit the states from exercising a power, then that power is in the hands of the states or the people. While specifically listing *rights* for the people does not limit these rights (Amendment IX), listing *government powers* is limiting. In both cases, the people are protected from the federal government using either kind of list to increase its power over them. Nevertheless, the "necessary and proper" clause (Article I, Section 8, Clause 18) ensures that governmental powers are not limited *too* strictly to a list. It allows the federal government to assume powers that it *implicitly* needs to adequately fulfill its duties. The precise limits of implied federal power are often debatable.

Some rights considered fundamental today were not originally affirmed. As only *citizens* could claim *civil rights* under the Constitution, slaves (who were treated as property) were denied all rights that a consistent application of the principle "all men are created equal" (Declaration of Independence) would imply. Moreover, the Constitution did not originally empower Congress to outlaw slavery, and the Tenth Amendment apparently gave states the right to decide on this issue for themselves. It was not until the 1860s that most African Americans were (at least theoretically) given equal constitutional rights by Amendments XIII, XIV and XV, and for many it would take yet another century for those rights to become a reality. Furthermore, the "right to vote" would first be mentioned in Amendment XIV, whereby race and gender discrimination in voting were officially outlawed by Amendments XV and IXX, respectively. As the Bill of Rights was originally only applied to limiting the *federal* government's power, Amendment XIV clarified that all the rights guaranteed to Americans have to be fully respected by the *state* governments as well. A special problem was the status of Native American tribes, which were systematically denied rights by both federal and state governments. Since they were treated as independent nations outside of the American system (cf. Article I, Section 2, Clause 3), the rights of citizens were not applied to them until Congress decided to do so in 1924.

8. Early Reforms and American Reconstruction (Amendments XI-XV)

The original Constitution, together with the Bill of Rights, has survived over two centuries. In this time, however, it has been significantly modified by seventeen further amendments. The first two of these reflect early attempts to improve the court system and presidential elections, respectively. Amendments XIII-XV, the *"Reconstruction Amendments"* ratified after the Civil War, established a dramatically new constitutional basis for the legal status and rights of African-Americans and other minorities. These amendments deal with freeing all slaves and guaranteeing basic liberties to "all persons." While Amendment XIII ended slavery and Amendment XV prohibited racial discrimination in voting, Amendment XIV guaranteed full citizenship and "equal protection" for African Americans. Beyond this intention, Amendment XIV also ended up having largely unforeseen implications for church-state relations, gun law, the national debt, state immunity from being sued, and illegal immigration! After providing a basis for *both* sides of the argument about racial segregation, it has encouraged women, various racial and ethnic minorities, and same-sex couples to demand "equal protection," expecting the federal government to step in and nullify unfair state laws. While the Bill of Rights had protected the people and states from the federal government, Amendment XIV gives Congress the role of protecting people from their own states.

Early Governmental Reforms (Amendments XI-XII)

In 1795, only three years after the Bill of Rights had taken effect, Amendment XI was ratified. It did not simply *add* to the Constitution but actually nullified two lines in the original text. According to Article III, Section 2, cases arising "between a State and Citizens of another State" or of a foreign country fall under the *federal* courts' jurisdiction. In 1793, a man from South Carolina won before the Supreme Court in a case against the state of Georgia. Many people did not like the idea that an outsider could force their state to court. Amendment XI thus added that those who are *not* citizens of a particular state – i.e., other Americans and foreign citizens or countries – *do not* have this right. Do citizens have a right to take *their own* state government to federal court? As neither Amendment XI nor Article III addresses this question, it is apparently left up to the states (cf. Amendment X), which themselves possess the right to review cases against them. Amendment XIV, however, would later change this in cases concerning the basic rights of all citizens (civil rights).

Amendment XII reacts against specific circumstances as well. In the election of 1800, running mates Thomas Jefferson and Aaron Burr received the same amount of electoral votes, as the delegates who supported both of them voted "for two Persons." Even though the two candidates intended to form a *team* of president and vice president, when they officially "tied" in the election, it was handed over to the House of Representatives. Amendment XII, ratified in 1804, sought to correct this problem so that presidential and vice presidential candidates could run together without being counted as opponents. Its text looks quite similar to the third paragraph of Article II, Section 1. Most of the basic procedure is simply repeated, but the statement that the electors vote "for two Persons" is corrected to read "for President and Vice President." No longer are they to simply make "a List," but rather two "distinct lists," one for electoral votes for president, and another for vice president.

In addition, if the House has to elect a president, it chooses between the top three candidates, not the top five as originally stated. Amendment XII also adds that simply having more electors than other candidates is no longer sufficient to become vice president; a *majority* is required. Otherwise, the Senate selects the vice president from the two candidates with the most electoral votes. According to the original plan, this would happen only if two candidates had tied.

Mirroring the House election of the president, the Senate is now also required to form a quorum (see Article II, Section 1, Clause 3), and a majority of senators must agree on the choice for vice president. This situation actually came about in the election of 1824; the House chose the *second* candidate, John Quincy Adams, as president, and the Senate chose his *opponent's* running mate, John Calhoun, as vice president! Whereas Article II only lists qualifications for the office of president, Amendment XII adds that the vice president has to fulfill the same requirements (natural born citizen, etc.). A potential problem is that Amendment XII gives the House of Representatives power to choose the president – if no candidate has a majority of electoral votes – just before its members' terms are over. As this puts a lot of power into the hands of representatives who may not have been re-elected by the people, it is corrected by Amendment XX.

The End of Slavery (Amendment XIII)

Amendments XI and XII included the first changes intended to correct errors in the Constitution, thus setting a precedent for making even greater modifications later. After Amendment XII was ratified, however, there were no further changes made to the Constitution for the next 61 years, the longest period that it has ever gone unmodified. In the meantime, the issue of slavery continued to polarize Americans. Opposition to slavery grew in the North, while support hardened in the South. As the southern states became increasingly intent on leaving the union, many northerners were willing to compromise on slavery in order to try to keep the country together. In 1861, an amendment written by northerners (!) was proposed that would have secured the rights of states over their "persons held to labor or service," making it impossible to add any further amendment empowering Congress to "abolish or interfere" with slavery. This attempt to appeal to the South by strengthening states' rights to regulate slavery was not enough to stop it from rebelling. Ironically, by declaring independence from the United States, the South in effect kept slave ownership from receiving new constitutional protection.

While the pro-slavery amendment proposed in 1861 went unratified, the Civil War opened up new possibilities. Halfway through the Civil War, President Lincoln declared ending slavery a new goal of the war and issued the Emancipation Proclamation of 1863, an executive order freeing slaves in rebelling states. This did not apply to the "border states" between North and South – the few slave states that supported the union – or to areas already under union control, and of course it was not enforced by the rebelling states. Even slaves that were now actually freed did not suddenly become American citizens or gain equal rights with whites. In addition, it was still possible for Congress or the Supreme Court to nullify this wartime measure and restore slavery everywhere. Many believed that Lincoln had gone beyond his constitutional authority as president, and planned to challenge and reverse his actions after the war. It seemed there was only one way to legally abolish slavery for good in the whole country – by amending the Constitution. As the southern states claimed to be independent and to form a new confederation, they were no longer sending representatives or senators to Congress. The northern-dominated Congress was then able (with difficulty) to pass a completely new amendment that did not protect slavery, but made it illegal. Once the South surrendered, it not only had to remain part of the United States, but to accept the end of slavery as well. The slave states that had not rebelled found themselves forced to do the same.

Once ratified, Amendment XIII marked a dramatic breakthrough in constitutional history. Slavery would no longer be tolerated even though the Constitution had originally permitted it. Instead of writing a new Constitution altogether (as some had proposed) two sentences were simply added. Doing away with slavery could then be understood not a *rejection* of the Constitution as a whole, but a necessary *correction* of it. The three-fifths rule (Article I, Section 2, Clause 3) was rendered void, because former slaves were now "free Persons," and nobody could be really considered part of "all other Persons" mentioned anymore. Of more immediate importance, Article IV, Section 2, could no longer be used to justify holding people to "Service or Labour" against their will. This had been the legal basis for considering slaves as property even if they escaped to states that did not recognize slavery. Against these statements, Amendment XIII declares:

> Neither slavery nor involuntary servitude, except as punishment for a crime whereof the party shall have been duly convicted, shall exist in the United States, or any place subject to their jurisdiction.

On the whole, surprisingly few words are at stake here. Amendment XIII makes one of the most powerful statements in American legal history, in a single sentence officially sweeping away a century of heated polarization and forced servitude. On the other hand, however, since it is so brief, it is not surprising that it failed to do near enough to provide full rights for the masses of slaves that were suddenly "freed" in a hostile environment. How were former slaves to now be integrated into the world of free people? For slaves who were now freed, life did not necessarily change as much as might be thought. Lacking education and facing harsh racism, many continued doing the same kind of labor as before (often for their former masters).

Amendment XIII did not specifically say that freed slaves would be treated as full and equal citizens, just that slavery would no longer exist. A long-term problem was that this did not bring about the end of racial segregation, which would continue to some extent for another century. Nor did it stop states from making laws targeted at keeping African Americans in a low position in society, as the end of slavery did not correspond to a change in mentality.

Rather than reflecting a new national consensus or a general development in moral sensitivity, Amendment XIII was pushed onto the southern states from the top down once they failed to gain independence and were defeated in the Civil War. It was approved shortly before the end of the war by a Congress in which they were not represented, and then new governments established by the Union (i.e., northern) forces in the southern states helped ratify it. Many southern whites then found ways to get around laws they felt had been illegally forced upon them.

Although Amendment XIII ends "involuntary servitude," it also allows an exception. The clause "…except as a punishment for crime…." presents the first and only time that the Constitution says that criminals can be forced to do work, clarifying that "cruel and unusual punishment" (Amendment VIII) does not forbid this practice. Alarmingly, this exception clause ended up providing a loophole for continuing to use former slaves for forced labor as long as they could be convicted of breaking a law. Laws were passed restricting blacks' movement, and if they violated these they could be convicted of "vagrancy" and forced to do slave-like labor as part of their prison sentence. Such cases went on in some former slave states into the early 20th century.

Finally, Section 2 of this amendment represents a new kind of clause that then sets a precedent followed by several later amendments. The first eleven amendments did not have a separate statement giving Congress "power to enforce" them. After the Civil War, many states did not want to apply Amendment XIII. As already seen, the Tenth Amendment gives all powers to the states that are not specifically given to Congress. When the powers of Congress are listed in Article I, Section 8, there is of course nothing there about ending slavery. Without adding section 2 to Amendment XIII, it could thus have been argued that Congress had no authority to make any laws actually *enforcing* the end of slavery, leaving this step up to the states. As the latter in turn might have simply taken no action, Congress was specifically given this additional power.

Equally Protected Citizens (Amendment XIV, Section 1)

In light of Amendment XIII's limitations, in 1868 Amendment XIV was added. This ambitious amendment, the longest in the Constitution, features new, sweeping statements on citizenship, voting rights, allocating Congress members, punishing rebels, and the national debt! Section 1 declares that all people born in the United States are automatically full citizens. Originally intended to ensure citizenship to former slaves, this guarantee would then later be applied to any children born in the country, even if their parents were illegal immigrants.

People who are "naturalized," i.e., immigrants who are granted citizenship, have the same rights as those born as citizens. The additional requirement of being "subject to the jurisdiction" of the United States excludes Native Americans subject to their own tribal laws. How exactly to become "naturalized" is not explained here, but is left up to Congress (Article I, Section 8, Clause 4). Congress had passed a law limiting naturalization to "free white persons," which was then expanded in 1870 to include "persons of African descent" as well (e.g., for those brought over prior to the end of the slave trade 40 years before). Native Americans and Asians were still not able to be naturalized. Congress did not grant citizenship to all Native Americans until 1924 and did not ban all racial discrimination in naturalization until 1952.

Civil rights, i.e., the basic rights of citizens, had already been guaranteed by the Bill of Rights, but these did not apply to slaves (non-citizens). Upon becoming citizens, newly freed people now had a legal claim to these very same rights. While the Declaration of Independence had named "life, liberty and the pursuit of happiness" as people's natural rights, the Fifth Amendment speaks of citizens' right to "life, liberty" and "property," which the federal government can only take away by "due process of law." The "pursuit of happiness" was substituted here by the more tangible concept of "property," which is easier to define by law. Most people of African origin in the United States were originally considered part of such "property." Citizens had a right to own property as defined by their own state, and that could include slaves. Amendments XIII and XIV placed former slaves into an entirely new legal category. Others no longer had a right to own them as property, but they now for the first time had a legal right to liberty and property themselves.

In this radically new legal context, Amendment XIV explicitly repeats the *due process* clause from the Fifth Amendment. It emphasizes that not only the *federal* government cannot deprive anyone "of life, liberty or property, without due process of law," but *state* governments cannot do so either. American citizens have to be given full rights as citizens *of their own state* as well, and states are not legally permitted to treat any of their citizens unfairly. Nobody, including African-Americans, can be denied the "privileges or immunities" enjoyed by other citizens. For example, blacks would have to be given the same rights as whites to freedom of speech, privacy, and a trial by jury.

After re-affirming the due process clause, Amendment XIV adds another one of the most significant and influential statements in American legal history concerning civil rights – the *equal protection clause*. It declares that no state is permitted "to deny to any person within its jurisdiction the equal protection of the laws." This meant that nobody could legally be kept from benefiting from the rights given to other citizens. For example, African Americans had to be allowed to get an education, and universities for them were in fact founded throughout the South following Reconstruction. A small number of blacks were elected to political offices, and a few even represented southern states in Congress in the latter part of the 19th century.

On the whole, however, the adoption of Amendment XIV was by itself not enough to truly ensure equal rights. The fact that it was added without a dramatic change in public mentality meant that blacks were not integrated into "white" society. Blacks now had a right to a jury trial, but the jury would be all white and presumably prejudiced. In theory they could move up in society, but then they faced the danger of being attacked by racist groups that the state may not really try to stop. Furthermore, the term "equal protection" allowed the argument that racial *segregation* could be "separate but equal" (*Plessy v. Ferguson* in 1896). In former slave states blacks and whites were still separated from each other in public facilities, transportation, schools and universities through over half of the 20th century. This constitutional guarantee of "equal protection" would, however, eventually lead to the end of racial segregation once the Supreme Court finally acknowledged that the practice promoted *in*equality (*Brown v. Board of Education*). It would also provide a strong constitutional foundation for the Civil Rights Movement in the 1950s and 1960s (see under Amendment XXIV).

The equal protection clause itself also paved the way for citizens to sue their own home state in federal courts. If a state could ignore its people's rights and then refuse to let them demand their rights in court, this could make Amendment XIV unenforceable. It would depend completely on the individual states to "enforce" the restrictions placed on them and they would be immune to any accusations that they were not doing so properly or quickly enough. This was a real concern, as the former slave states often resisted the idea of treating African-Americans in the same way as white citizens. By guaranteeing all citizens *protection from their own state*, Amendment XIV provided a constitutional basis for citizens to bring their own state to court, a situation that had not yet foreseen by Amendment XI. In particular, citizens could accuse their state of not giving them true *equal protection* or fully protecting their *civil rights*, the rights common to all citizens. In the 20th century, the Supreme Court ended up playing a central role in (re-)defining equal protection for African Americans as well as for other racial minorities.

In addition, Amendment XIV puts some of the previous amendments in a new light. For example, it boosts arguments both for restricting states from supporting religion or limiting individual gun rights. Although the First Amendment begins with "Congress shall...", together with Amendment XIV, "equal protection" can now be applied to religion at the state level as well. States cannot support Christianity in a way that implies less than equal protection for religious minorities. Similarly, states have more difficulty restricting weapons, as the Second Amendment is now seen as a right protecting citizens not only from federal laws, but from their own states as well.

The equal protection clause has been at the center of debates over same sex-marriage and abortion. It was clear that states could recognize same sex unions as "marriage." But do they have to? Do states have a right to determine how they define marriage? That is, can states show preference to traditional marriage unions (e.g., by granting tax benefits) due to the belief that these are beneficial to society, providing an ideal situation for children to be born and raised? Until recently, this was legally the case. However, according to the Supreme Court ruling in 2015, "equal protection" gives same-sex couples a right to all the benefits of married opposite-sex couples, such as equal tax benefits, the ability to adopt children, and the official designation of "marriage." Another very controversial issue is abortion. If unborn children are considered "*persons*" while still within the womb, then they should also receive "equal protection" and have a basic right to life. Especially once fetuses have developed to the stage where they could possibly survive if they were outside of their mothers, many states have laws sympathetic to this viewpoint. On the other hand, according to the 1973 Supreme Court decision *Roe v. Wade*, as abortion has to do with a woman's choice about developments inside her own body, it is legally protected under personal privacy rights.

The Right to Vote (Amendments XIV, XV)

Amendment XIV includes four additional sections clarifying the right to vote as well as other issues in the post-war situation. First of all, granting citizenship to former slaves had to effect the political process and voting. In Amendment XIV, Section 2, the three-fifths rule, already negated by Amendment XIII, is officially replaced. There is no longer any distinction between "free Persons" and "all other Persons" (Article I, Section 2, Clause 3). Since this time, representatives have been assigned based simply on the total "number of persons" in the respective state (as before excluding Indians). Going a step further, male citizens were granted a fundamental "right to vote" upon turning 21 years old. At least in theory, this included black men who had recently before been slaves. In reality, however, states often made it difficult for them to make use of this right. Women would have to wait over 50 more years for such a guarantee (see under Amendment XIX). While most white men could in fact vote at this point, the Constitution had never actually guaranteed this as a right before. In accord with Amendment X, determining who exactly could vote had been left up to the states.

Finally, a penalty was placed on states for not enforcing this new constitutional right. If any adult male citizens, including black men, are denied the "right to vote" for any federal or state office, then they will not be counted as part of the population for determining the total number of representatives for the state. This penalty system is not fully satisfying. It seems that states were technically permitted to deny the vote to black men as long as these states were willing to accept the penalty of not having representatives to represent their black communities in Congress! The wording in Amendment XIV, Section 2, is clearly supposed to stop racial discrimination in voting, but it fails to really get to the point.

Sections 3 and 4 of Amendment XIV focus on how to deal with those who had rebelled in the Civil War. Section 3 denies the right to hold any public office to anyone who (a) swore an oath to be faithful to the Constitution in the government or military, and (b) despite this oath supported a rebellion, i.e., the Southern attempt to leave the United States. Although Section 3 requires two-thirds of Congress to lift this ban, the many former Confederate (i.e., southern rebel) leaders who had already been pardoned by the president could continue to hold office. Furthermore, as Congress was responsible for enforcing this (Section 5), former rebels could stay in office until Congress actually removed them. Rather than enforce this ban strictly, Congress gave up on it altogether, and finally officially declared it void in 1898. The directive to give states less representatives if they kept blacks from voting was never enforced by Congress either. These examples show how strongly constitutional guarantees depend on the government actually implementing them. The same can be said for "equal protection" and the right to vote, which for many did not become a reality until the Civil Rights Era or even later.

Amendment XIV, Section 4, nullifies any attempt to demand repayment from the government for freed slaves or for any losses incurred due to rebelling. For the first time, the Constitution gives the government a right to a "public debt." The statement that the "validity of the public debt…. shall not be questioned" was provoked by the debt from the Civil War, but this would also justify any future debt the government might have. Relating this to current politics, does Amendment XIV prohibit setting a debt ceiling, saying that the government cannot incur any more than a certain amount of debt? Or does the phrase "authorized by law" indicate that Congress can make a law limiting debt, whereas debt beyond that is not protected?

As Amendment XIV did not do enough to ensure equal voting rights, the brief Amendment XV, ratified almost two years later in 1870, goes a step further in explicitly forbidding both federal and state government from keeping anyone from voting due to "race, color, or previous condition of servitude." This seems pretty clear. And yet, even this statement was more limited in effect than it might seem. No discrimination against African Americans or former slaves was allowed in voting, but what about in other areas of public life? Furthermore, not allowing citizens to vote was still allowed for other reasons (such as gender), just not due to race or previously having been a slave. Many states set up requirements for voting that did not officially discriminate for these reasons. For example, states were able to keep people from voting who could not pass a test or afford a poll tax, effectively keeping the illiterate and poor from voting, and limiting the black vote. In addition, states passed "grandfather clauses" that gave exemptions to men whose grandfathers had voted, meaning for instance that they could vote without first having to take a difficult test. It would take about an entire century to make sure that the black population as a whole even began to have fair opportunity to take full advantage of the right to vote promised here in theory. The full fruit of Amendments XIV and XV would not be ripe until much, much later. In the end, they would serve as the constitutional basis for the *Civil Rights* Movement as well as court decisions and legislation associated with it (see under Amendment XXIV).

9. The Early 20th Century (Amendments XVI-XXI)

Over four decades after the Restoration Amendments freed slaves and officially gave African Americans equal rights, it became clear that the Constitution would continue to grow in the 20th century. The main themes of the twelve amendments added in this period are reforming the government and expanding voting rights. For the most part they modify the Constitution's first two articles, affecting Congress and the presidency. The first six of these were ratified within a twenty year time period in three groups of two in 1913, 1919-1920, and 1933, respectively. In the optimistic spirit of the "Progressive Era," the first two pairs attempted to improve society. In Amendments XVI to XIX, the "Progressive Era Amendments," industrialists were taxed, democracy was expanded, alcohol sales were stopped, and women gained the right to vote. After the prosperous 1920s ended, the Constitution was then again amended during the Great Depression to improve transitions to newly elected governments and to make alcohol legal again.

Power to the People (Amendments XVI-XVII)

Amendment XVI says that Congress can "lay and collect taxes on incomes, from whatever source derived." An amendment here might seem unnecessary, as Article I, Section 8, Clause 1 had already given Congress the "Power To lay and collect Taxes." The language, however, is directed against Article I, Section 9, Clause 4, which forbid a "direct Tax" on citizens themselves that was not based strictly on population ("No… direct, Tax …unless in proportion to the Census or Enumeration…"). Sales tax is considered *indirect*, since the tax is on the product being sold, not on the person buying it, and this was the main source of income for the government before Amendment XVI. Even a tax based on income, targeted at people who earn a lot of money, was permitted by the courts, which saw this as taxing the *work*, not the worker. However, taxing people for money earned from interest was especially problematic, because the tax targeted certain *people* (i.e., investors, property owners) so the federal government could simply take some of their money. There was a strong argument that people could not be taxed more than others just because they earned interest from their own money or their own property. This position was beneficial for industrialists (who earned money from interest), and most people in less industrial areas found it unfair. When Amendment XVI was ratified in 1913, this represented a re-integration of the (more rural) South into the country, as it played a leading role in pushing the amendment through.

Amendment XVII was ratified just two months after Amendment XVI and was seen as yet another victory for the common people. Senators were no longer to be "chosen by the Legislature" of their respective state (Article I, Section 3, Clause 1), but "elected by the people." This major reform in government made senators directly accountable to the voters. In addition, the second clause of Amendment XVII directs state governors ("the executive authority") to call a special election giving the people the opportunity to elect a new senator if a seat becomes vacant, i.e., because a senator resigns, is impeached, or dies. Until such an election takes place, the governor can still "make temporary appointments" (as already stated in Article I, Section 3, Clause 2), but only if the state legislature permits. The term "temporary" is not defined exactly; some states' legislatures interpret this to be any period under two years. On the whole, state legislatures lost power due to Amendment XVII. They no longer have influence outside their state, as they no longer appoint anyone to represent them in the capital. Moreover, senators now tend to focus more on national issues and less on their state governments' interests.

Besides this fundamental change, the other differences between the two chambers remain. The Senate's basic function of keeping the House of Representatives in check on the one hand, and the executive branch on the other hand, is preserved. Moreover, senators still represent all states equally regardless of population, serve longer terms than representatives (six years instead of two), make up a smaller body (100 compared to 435), and approve treaties and appointed positions made by the president. The Senate is thus still seen as the "upper," more prestigious house. It should be noted here that "the people" mentioned in Amendment XVII is still defined as those who can vote ("the electors") for the larger (i.e., lower) law-making body in their own state. According to Amendment XIV, this would have to include all male citizens 21 years of age and above. Depending on the state, women could be included as part of the voting population as well, but there was no nation-wide, constitutional protection for women's right to vote until 1920 (see under Amendment XIX). Native Americans and Asian immigrants were denied citizenship, while literacy tests and poll taxes were used to keep many citizens (especially blacks) from exercising this right (see under Amendment XXIV).

Purchasing Alcohol (Amendments XVIII, XXI)

In the early 20th century, many Americans were very optimistic about their ability to change society for the better. The people were empowered by Amendments XVI and XVII, and the movement for women's voting rights was steadily making progress. Besides these issues, many believed that it was also time to move beyond the addictive and destructive behavior associated with drinking alcohol, which was widely considered to be the main cause of poverty and violence. Amendment XVIII introduced Prohibition, making it illegal to "manufacture, sale," transport, import or export "intoxicating liquors." Interestingly, it does not actually say anything about *consuming* alcoholic beverages. The specification "for beverage purposes" is included, thus permitting wine to still be used in religious ceremonies (free exercise clause, Amendment I).

An innovative feature of Amendment XVIII is setting specific *time limits*. It would not take effect immediately, but after it was ratified at the beginning of the year 1919, Americans were permitted to buy alcoholic beverages for exactly one year. Some purchased very large amounts so they could continue drinking from what they had in storage once Prohibition took effect. Moreover, for the first time there is a requirement of being *ratified within a seven year period*. Article V does not mention any such time limit, but it does not rule out the concept either. In contrast to all previous amendments, if Amendment XVIII had not been ratified within seven years, then if would have expired and could not have become part of the Constitution. Another unique feature is that Section 2 gives *both* Congress and the states the ability to make laws enforcing Prohibition ("concurrent power"). The Restoration Amendments depended on Congress alone, as the former slave states were not trusted to apply them. Amendment XVIII, however, specifically gives states the right to make their own anti-alcohol laws in addition to – and possibly more quickly and strictly than – the laws Congress might make.

Amendment XVIII is the only amendment in the Constitution targeted at *taking away* a personal liberty. While Amendment XVII could possibly be seen as taking away the liberty to not be taxed on money made on interest or property, this was really about closing a loophole in the original Constitution. One could perhaps construe Amendment XIII as taking away the liberty of people to own slaves, but the purpose is clearly to *expand* liberty, giving a large group of people freedom and simply stopping others from continuing to restrict this. As alcohol abuse can be detrimental to society and families, many were convinced that the freedom to buy and sell a substance thought to be so destructive should be restricted. This sentiment was not unique to the United States. The "temperance" movement against alcohol was a strong force internationally, although it prevailed in only a relatively small number of countries. Canada, Iceland, Finland and Norway all banned the sale of alcohol shortly before the United States did. Other countries had partial restrictions at that time, e.g., in Russia alcohol could only be consumed in restaurants.

In the United States, as elsewhere, the experiment of Prohibition was well-intentioned, but ultimately not successful; alcohol was simply bought and sold *illegally*, creating even more problems. As Amendment XVIII kept alcohol laws from being loosened, there was only one way out – adding yet another amendment. In 1933, Amendment XXI was ratified, stating that Amendment XVIII "is hereby repealed," thus stripping it of its constitutional authority. Though parts of the original Constitution have been nullified by later amendments many times, this is the only instance in which one amendment has canceled out another one.

Section 2 of Amendment XXI reformulated a new "prohibition" law, declaring that it is still illegal to bring "intoxicating liquor" anywhere where it is prohibited. Is an amendment really needed to tell us that alcohol is not allowed in any place where it is not allowed? The point was that repealing Amendment XVIII does not automatically legalize alcoholic beverages, nor does it give Americans any constitutional right to buy or sell them. Rather, Amendment XXI removes *national* prohibition and leaves the matter up to the states, some of which continued to restrict intoxicating drinks. Since 1966, however, all the states have permitted buying and selling alcohol again. Nevertheless, even today there are hundreds of "dry counties," areas within some states where alcohol sales are restricted. Such laws do not prohibit consuming drinks purchased outside the respective county, nor do they rule out producing alcoholic beverages to be sold elsewhere. A famous dry county is Moore County, Tennessee, where Jack Daniel's whiskey is produced. Legally, alcoholic drinks can be *made* there as long as they are only marketed and *sold* elsewhere. Since 1984, buying alcohol has been restricted in the whole country before the age of 21, but once again the details concerning alcohol laws can vary widely from state to state. Contrary to a common misconception, most states allow people under 21 to *drink* (but not to *buy*) alcoholic beverages in certain circumstances, e.g., in private or at least with their families.

The last sentence in Amendment XXI looks at first glance like an exact copy of Section 3 in Amendment XVIII, saying that the amendment will expire if not ratified within seven years. A closer look reveals a unique feature. Instead of being ratified "by the legislatures of the several states," Amendment XXI was to be ratified "by conventions in the several states." The first step, proposing the amendment, was done as usual by Congress, but the second step required *state ratifying conventions*. This possibility is given in Article V, but Amendment XXI is the only one to have ever actually been ratified in this way.

Amendments XVIII and XXI still remain in the Constitution, as there is no procedure for actually removing something from it. These two amendments reflect an unusual, experimental chapter in constitutional history. Amendment XVIII shows that the Constitution can be amended to take away a liberty, even one that had always been allowed before, and even if directed against a specific group of people (in this case, drinkers). A lasting effect of Amendment XVIII was its seven year time limit for ratification, setting a precedent that was followed in Amendments XX, XXI, and XXII, as well as in two other amendments that were successfully proposed, but not ratified by the deadline. One guaranteeing equal rights regardless of sex expired in 1982, while another one that would have given the District of Columbia representation in Congress expired in 1985. Amendment XXI in turn demonstrates that an earlier amendment is not necessarily permanent, but can be nullified. Even statements in the Bill of Rights (some might think of the Second Amendment here) could be repealed. Moreover, Amendment XXI sets a potential precedent for using state ratifying conventions to approve amendments.

Voting Rights for Women (Amendment XIX)

Since the middle of the 19th century, there had been a significant movement in favor of extending voting rights to American women. A founding document was the Declaration of Sentiments (put forward at the Seneca Falls Convention in 1848), a cleverly formulated text based on the Declaration of Independence. It proclaims: "We hold these truths to be self-evident: that all men and women are created equal." Furthermore, in place of the British king who denied Americans their rights, men are condemned for unjustly depriving women of equal treatment. In particular, excluding women from the political process is emphasized – every woman has to "submit to laws, in the formation of which she has no voice." Furthermore, it objects to women not being given rights concerning property, divorce or education. Such problems with the law could be improved, however, if women could only *vote*, thus having an influence on issues important to them. Gaining this right would take several decades of devotion to the cause.

Since Amendments XIV and XV were ratified, all adult men have had a constitutional right to vote, at least in theory. In reality, it still remained possible to indirectly keep large numbers of African-Americans from voting by demanding poll taxes and literacy tests (not officially due to race; see under Amendment XXIV). At the same time, in declaring a "right to vote" for "male inhabitants," Amendment XIV introduced the first reference to sex in the Constitution. The declaration of citizens' rights to black men also represents the first explicit *exclusion* of women from these full rights. Furthermore, Amendment XV rules out voting discrimination based on race, but *not* on sex. The struggle for *women's suffrage* (i.e., equal voting rights) thus had to be dealt with on the state level. As issues not addressed in the Constitution are left up to the states (Amendment X), Congress did not have any authority to interfere with whether or not women could vote in the states. Nevertheless, Congress did manage to interfere in Utah as long as it was still a *territory* under federal control but not yet an actual "state." Women there could vote as early as 1869, but this right was taken away from them by Congress in 1887, and re-gained once Utah was admitted as a state in 1896. By the end of the 19th century, women had equal voting rights with men in four states, all in the West (Wyoming, Colorado, Utah, Idaho). As the movement gained more momentum, women obtained full voting rights in twelve additional states between 1910 and 1918, and in thirteen others they could at least vote in presidential elections by this time.

In order to make a nation-wide law protecting women's suffrage, a new addition to the Constitution was necessary. Despite initial resistance in the Senate, this was finally ratified in 1920 as Amendment IXX. The wording is identical to that of Amendment XV, except that it reads "on account of sex" in the place of "on account of race, color, or previous condition of servitude." This word-for-word repetition points out that women had previously been denied voting rights as slaves had been before. Although women (at least white women) had always been citizens, they had not been given the same civil rights as men, not having been allowed to fully participate in the democratic process.

After gaining the right to vote in all elections, opportunities for women themselves to be elected to public office increased as well. The first woman had already entered the House of Representatives in 1917, and following Amendment XIX women from regions all over the country have served in the House in slowly but steadily increasing numbers. In the 1920s, the states of Wyoming and Texas had female governors, while in the 1930s four women served in the Senate. In the mid-20th century, however, the presence of women in politics declined; only a few more women entered the Senate and none served as governors, but since the 1970s a significant number of women have obtained these positions. Since the 1980s, there has always been at least one woman on the Supreme Court. Since the 1990s, three women have served as the president's Secretary of State. In the 21st century, for the first time, Americans have had a female Speaker of the House.

Beyond the equal voting rights guaranteed by Amendment XIX, there were attempts to go a step further and introduce yet another amendment making any form of sex discrimination illegal. Finally, the Equal Rights Amendment (ERA, 1972) proposed adding: "Equality of rights under the law shall not be denied or abridged by the United States or any State on account of sex." Although this passed in both houses of Congress, it failed to be ratified by three fourths of the states. Much of the opposition was due to concerns about what "equality" would mean. If no legal distinction could be made between men and women, would it still be possible to demand husbands to take financial responsibility for dependent wives, provide special protection for mothers, exempt women from being drafted to the military, or make laws directed at sex crimes against women? Some women believed that an amendment demanding complete gender equality would be a milestone in favor of women's rights, but others feared that the ERA could actually end legal protection specifically for women. Of course, many laws are discussed and made today in the interest of gender equality, for example, in the workplace. These are dealt with, however, by acts of Congress and by state laws, as well as by court decisions, but not by a new amendment.

Reforms in Governmental Procedure (Amendment XX)

In the year 1933 two unrelated amendments were ratified in the midst of the hardships of the Great Depression. While the year closed with Amendment XXI ending Prohibition in December, in January it had begun with Amendment XX introducing reforms to the government. Amendment XX attempts to better organize the schedule of taking federal offices. It is particularly concerned with dates, specifying exactly when terms end and when Congress has to meet. A unique feature is specifying a date for particular sections of the amendment to be applied (in October before elections in November), whereby the remaining sections would take effect immediately after being ratified. Since the first Congress began meeting on March 4 (in 1789), this date continued to serve as the starting point for congressional terms, and soon for presidential terms as well. This date is not mentioned in the Constitution until Amendment XII, which gives the House of Representatives until March 4 to choose a president if no candidate receives a majority of electoral votes. As elections were held in November, representatives who had not been re-elected could vote for a new president if no candidate had a majority of electors. They also had a few months to vote on new laws before leaving office. This all seems to give too much power to people who have been voted out of office. In addition, advances in technology such as the telegram ensured that election results would be clear much sooner than ever before. Such a large time gap between elections and taking office did not make as much sense in 1933 as it may have in 1789.

Section 1 of Amendment XX establishes a clear procedure for the first month of the year. The senators and representatives begin their terms on January 3, and afterwards, on January 20, the president and vice president will be sworn in to their terms under the newly elected Congress. In section 2, the required meeting date for Congress is moved from the first Monday of December (Article I, Section 4, Clause 2) to January 3. The precise point when one congressional term officially ends and the next begins is 12:00 noon. The newly elected Congress is required to meet exactly at the very beginning of its term, at noon on January 3. Otherwise, both the requirement for Congress to meet at least once a year and the possibility for it to change the date of this mandatory meeting remain the same. It is rather strange that a specific date is mentioned, as the original formulation "the first Monday" is more practical. Now Congress has to meet on the weekend if January 3 happens to fall on a Saturday or Sunday, unless it specifically votes to move the date.

Sections 3 and 4 deal with what happens if no presidential candidate is elected in time, or if an elected president dies. Section 3 repeats the rule that vice president then takes over for the president, while specifying that the newly elected vice president ("Vice President elect") is meant, and specifically mentioning the case of an elected president dying before taking office. It is also possible, however, that the vice president elect could die as well. Moreover, one or more of the candidates could die before Congress has selected a president or vice president. If no candidate receives a majority of electors, what happens if then neither a president nor a vice president is successfully elected by a majority in the House or Senate? These are all theoretical problems that are not solved in the Constitution. Would Congress have the right to do anything about this, or would this leave an unclear and chaotic situation? Here, Amendment XX explicitly gives Congress the power to make laws dealing with such circumstances. Furthermore, if the problem is that no candidate qualifies in time, then any appointments to fulfill the empty presidential position are only temporary "until a President or Vice President shall have qualified."

In any case, since the date when the president is supposed to take office is over two weeks after the new Congress meets, members of the newly elected Congress (not members of Congress who are *leaving* office) will be responsible for dealing with any problems that come up regarding who should assume the office of president. Fortunately, this has never been necessary. Congress has, however, clarified in advance by law that if there is no living president or vice president able to act as the leader of the executive branch, the Speaker of the House of Representatives would assume this role (Presidential Succession Act of 1947). It has further clarified that the President pro Tempore of the Senate would act as president if the Speaker of the House was not able to, and then the fifteen leaders of executive departments are listed in order as being next in line. Should several government leaders ever suddenly be captured or killed, at least it will be clear who assumes the presidential position.

10. Further Modifications (Amendments XXII-XXVII)

After the United States had come out of the Great Depression and established itself as a global superpower in the Second World War, six more amendments were ratified in the second half of the 20th century. These additions make for a total of 27 amendments in the Constitution as it now stands. Amendments XXII-XXVII focus mainly on the presidential office and on voting. These reforms started with limits on presidents' time in office in 1951 (XXII) and ended with limits on Congress' pay in 1992 (XXVII). In between these two, four amendments were added from 1961 to 1971 amidst the Black Civil Rights Movement and the Vietnam War. These amendments expanded voting rights for residents of the capital city (XXIII), the poor (XXIV), and young adults (XXVI), and also made clearer when the vice president can assume the president's position (XXV). Altogether, Amendments XXII-XXVII represent attempts to further improve how America's *democratic system* of *representative government* works.

Presidential Elections (Amendments XXII, XXIII)

After Prohibition ended, the Constitution remained unchanged throughout the rest of Franklin D. Roosevelt's presidency (1933 to 1945), who won four consecutive elections. Though he was among the most popular and important presidents ever, his presidency was especially long and powerful. The fact that one person could gain such a dominant position seemed to conflict with the ideal of separating powers. For example, if a president is in office long enough, he could appoint the entire Supreme Court. In 1951, Amendment XXII added official term limits. Since then, nobody can be elected president for more than two terms, or for more than one term if he served over half of another person's term (i.e., if the vice-president takes over when a president dies or steps down). This rule is based on the example of George Washington and many other presidents who chose to retire from office and not run again after having served two terms. Amendment XXII made this traditional model into a legal requirement, thereby limiting the power and influence that any individual commander-in-chief can have. Presidents who are elected to a second term know that they are serving their last four years in office. On the one hand, they are freed up to concentrate on policies without worrying about an upcoming election. On the other hand, their political opponents are glad that a definite end is in sight. The remaining text exempts whoever was president when this amendment was proposed; that was Harry Truman, but he did not run for a third term.

In 1961, a decade after presidential term limits had been set, Amendment XXIII was ratified. It permits the capital city, Washington, D.C., to take part in presidential elections. The number of electoral delegates is based on the number of senators and representatives it *would* have if it were a state. This means a total of *three* delegates, as a single city would probably not have more than one representative. Even theoretically, regardless of population, the District of Columbia cannot have more electors "than the least populous state."

The status of people permanently living in Washington, D.C. has always been unusual. Though living in the city where Congress meets, they themselves cannot have representatives or senators, because they do not belong to a state. In 1978 Congress approved an amendment to treat the District "as though it were a State," giving it representation in Congress. However, this was not ratified by enough states within the seven-year time limit. Many Americans approve of the capital city having an independent, non-political status outside of the state system, but citizens there often complain that they are not fairly represented.

Abolishing the Poll Tax (Amendment XXIV)

In 1964, almost a century after the Restoration Amendments, a further amendment to protect voting rights was ratified. Poll taxes had long been used in many states as a barrier for poorer people to participate in elections. Finally, Amendment XXIV ensured a "right of citizens" to vote in all elections for federal offices – for president and vice president and their electors, as well as for senators and representatives. Elections for state offices were not addressed, but Amendment XIV would provide the legal basis for overruling poll taxes in state elections as well.

Amendment XXIV includes the Constitution's first reference to "primaries," elections within a party. Winning a primary only means becoming the candidate for a *party*, not being elected to an actual office. As many regions and states in the country strongly favor one of the two major parties over the other, primaries often determine who will probably win the general election. Well into the 20th century, the Democratic Party – for a long time the dominant party in the South – had allowed "white only" *primaries* in many states, thus keeping blacks from helping select who the Democratic candidates would be. (The Democratic Party has distanced itself sharply from such former positions and today strongly supports civil rights for minorities.) Although this practice had been outlawed by the Supreme Court in 1944 on the basis of Amendment XV, poll taxes could still be used to deter the poor (including large numbers of African Americans) in both primaries and general elections. Amendment XXIV outlawed this practice once and for all.

It may seem surprising that Amendment XXIV is the only amendment made in the civil rights era clearly aimed at removing a barrier to African Americans, and that no civil rights issues other than the poll tax problem are addressed. The other three amendments made in the 1950s and 1960s are all concerned with issues surrounding the presidency. In any case, the constitutional prohibition on demanding people to pay so they can vote represents an important civil rights victory. The most significant legal breakthroughs of the Civil Rights Movement, however, are found in court decisions and in laws passed by Congress. The government did not need to promote a series of new amendments, but to more fully apply and protect the civil rights that the Reconstruction Amendments had theoretically promised.

In 1954 the Supreme Court reversed the "separate but equal" doctrine that it had supported in 1896 (*Plessy v. Ferguson*), observing that this had not worked in practice and that "separate educational facilities are inherently unequal" (*Brown v. Board of Education*). School segregation was thus ruled to violate Amendment XIV's *equal protection* clause. Black children were not given "equal protection" under the law if they were kept out of white schools. The court argued that this kind of segregation based on skin color put black children at a disadvantage and promoted a sense of being worth less than white children. In the end, what exactly "equal protection" meant was determined by the Supreme Court, originally by allowing "separate but equal" schools, and then finally by outlawing segregation that promoted racial *in*equality.

A further, decisive step was the Civil Rights Act of 1964, which banned racial segregation in businesses and public places as well as racial discrimination in employment. However, just as Amendment XIV needed to be supplemented by Amendment XV to offer more (theoretical) protection of voting rights, the Civil Rights Act of 1964 did not go far enough in this regard either. The Voting Rights Act passed by Congress shortly afterwards in 1965 outlawed using a "voting qualification or prerequisite to voting" to keep people from participating in elections due to race (Section 2). This meant practices such as literacy tests were now ruled out. The legal loopholes found in the Reconstruction Amendments were closed. With these two acts, Congress finally managed to pass lasting "appropriate legislation" (Amendment XIV, Section 5; Amendment XV, Section 2) to enforce "equal protection" (Amendment XIV,

Section 1) and the "right of citizens of the United States to vote" (Amendment XV, Section 1), albeit a whole century later.

Not surprisingly, attempts to stop segregation raised objections about the federal government violating states' rights to regulate their own schools, transportation and businesses themselves. Besides pointing to Congress' right to enforce "equal protection" (Amendment XIV), proponents of civil rights also appealed to the commerce clause (Article I, Section 8, Clause 3). The Supreme Court ended up agreeing that the federal government is allowed to outlaw discrimination in transportation systems that cross state lines, as well as in businesses that serve significant numbers of people from other states or that buy articles from other states.

Replacing a President (Amendment XXV)

After outlawing poll taxes for electing federal offices in 1964, Amendment XXV was ratified in 1967. Beyond what had already been stated in Amendment XX, this clarified in more detail what happens if the president dies, resigns or is removed. The original wording was that the vice president takes over the "Powers and Duties" of the president in such cases (Article II, Section 1, Clause 6). Section 1 of Amendment XXV made explicit that the vice president does not only "act" in the deceased president's place, but actually *becomes* president. The eighth time this situation arose in American history was when President Kennedy was assassinated in 1963, and Lyndon B. Johnson was sworn in as president. Moreover, once Johnson became president, there was no vice president anymore. Section 2 of Amendment XXV says that in such a case, the president has to nominate someone to fill this empty position. If both the Senate and the House approve, this person becomes vice president. Section 3 clarifies that if a president officially announces that he is unable to act as president, the vice president takes over his "powers and duties" without *becoming* president. In contrast to when a president dies or leaves office, this is *temporary*. The president can still announce in writing that he is able to act as president again, and then he takes his "powers and duties" back from the vice president.

What if the president is not able to fulfill his duties, but is not able to officially announce this either? For example, the president could be in a coma or be captured. It seems that nobody would be able to act as president in this scenario. Amendment XXV, Section 4, allows the vice president to declare (once again, in writing to the Senate and House) the president's inability, and then he shall "immediately assume the powers and duties of the office as Acting President." The vice president cannot do this all alone, but needs the support of the majority of the executive officers. Today, that would mean at least eight out of fifteen cabinet members. Congress can also appoint another group to make this decision, thus covering the case of the executive officers not being able to. The president then assumes his powers again once he officially submits a statement.

An additional, new feature introduced by Amendment XXV is that the vice president and the executive officers (or "another body" appointed by Congress) can try to remove the president against his will. If the president declares that he can fulfill his duties, but the vice president and over half the officers (who were appointed by the president!) disagree with this statement, then Congress decides between the president and the vice president. Perhaps a president could claim to be able to properly exercise the powers of his office when he really is not fit to. This means there is now another theoretical way to remove a president besides the traditional impeachment procedure. The vice president can manage to simply replace the president if he can get the majority of the executive department leaders and Congress to support him. To date nothing like this has ever been attempted.

In short, Amendment XXV represents an effort to think through every possible scenario that could go wrong, ensuring that the

United States will always have a clear commander-in-chief. Questions that had not been clearly answered before – or even seriously asked – are now covered in minute detail. A single line in the original Constitution is clarified with an entire new page. It is not surprising that an amendment reflecting this kind of concern was passed at the height of the Cold War and after a president had been assassinated.

Voting Age and Congress' Pay (Amendments XXVI, XXVII)

Amendment XXVI, ratified in 1971, lowers the minimum voting age to 18 years old; under Amendment XIV it had been age 21. Amendment XXVI uses the same basic wording as Amendments XV and IXX. It repeats "The right of citizens of the United States …to vote shall not be denied or abridged...", but adds "who are eighteen years of age or older" and says "on account of age" instead of "on account of race, color, or previous condition of servitude," or "on account of sex." This was passed very easily, and was ratified by the state legislatures within just four months, the quickest this has ever happened. It is not surprising that there was such strong support in the midst of the deadly conflict in Vietnam – it seemed unfair that 18 year olds could be drafted to fight in the military and told they have to risk their lives, but did not have a right to participate in elections like adults. There appears to be a trend here, with voting rights being extended due to war experiences. Black men gained the right to vote after the Civil War, women after supporting their country in the First World War, and young people between 18 and 21 towards the end of the war in Vietnam.

Although the purpose of Amendment XXVI is clearly to extend a "right of citizens …to vote" to Americans between 18 and 21 years of age, the language used rules out any voter discrimination "on account of age." It is not possible for people to be denied a right to vote for being too old either. Together with Amendments XV and

IXX, this completes a threefold constitutional guarantee for all Americans to vote in all state and federal elections without being discriminated against due to *race, sex or age*. The Constitution does not, however, say that voting rights cannot be taken away for other reasons. In particular, criminals can have their liberties taken away, including the right to vote (due process clause). Moreover, Americans are required to *register* to vote; failing to do so before a set date is a legally accepted reason to be barred from voting.

A rather odd feature of the Constitution is that its most recent amendment is also its oldest one – the original "First" Amendment proposed in 1789 was not ratified until 1992! The Constitution already made clear that senators and representatives are compensated by federal funds, while how much they are paid is "to be ascertained by Law" (Article I, Section 6, Clause 1), i.e., this is determined by Congress itself. Since members of Congress could be tempted to dramatically increase their own wages, James Madison had proposed an amendment as part of the Bill of Rights that would limit members of Congress from raising (or lowering) their own pay ("varying the compensation"). It would only allow pay changes to take effect once a new House of Representatives took office, i.e., every two years. The first Congress accepted this limitation on its own power. Nevertheless, some argued that this would make it impossible for Congressmen to lower their *own* pay, but they could reduce the pay of those coming into office *after* them. Finally, this amendment, failing to gain the required three fourths of the states, was largely forgotten.

Much later, a movement arose raising concerns about Congress repeatedly increasing its pay. In the 1980s more and more states ratified this amendment and in 1992 it had gained the three fourths of states required, thus becoming part of the Constitution. This highly unusual incident was possible since the Constitution does not set any time limit for amendments to be ratified. The actual effect of Amendment XXVII is minimal, as members of Congress continue to benefit from annual pay increases (to adjust for the cost of living) established before their term. More important is the symbolic significance of passing the amendment and the implications it has for the amendment process.

There are three (or four) additional "forgotten" amendments proposed by Congress long ago that apparently could still be ratified. Madison actually brought twelve articles of amendment before Congress: In addition to the Bill of Rights ratified in 1791 and Amendment XXVII, he put forth an amendment (which Congress accepted) saying that one representative could not represent more than 50,000 people, keeping the membership of the House from ever falling below 200. Other successfully proposed amendments that were never ratified would cause Americans who accept titles of nobility or gifts from foreign governments to lose their citizenship, and would explicitly give Congress power to restrict child labor. These were proposed in 1810 and 1926, respectively. A proposal protecting "domestic institutions" (i.e., slavery) is still technically open as well, though since Amendment XIII this has no longer been an issue. At the present time, there are no newly proposed amendments waiting to be ratified. Moreover, in the current, deeply divided political climate, there is not likely to be an issue that enough Americans demand adding to the Constitution and that would also be able to gain the large majorities in Congress and the states demanded by Article V. The most controversial legal questions in America today revolve around how to interpret the Constitution as it already stands.

Outlook: Constitutional Law

This commentary has now guided the reader step-by-step through the entire Constitution, from the original articles drafted by the framers in 1787 to the ratification of Amendment XXVII in 1992. We have at last reached the end, which may also be seen as a new beginning, a solid foundation to build upon. For a start, the reader should be able to understand many current issues addressed in the daily news on a deeper level, both today and in the years to come.

Those interested in the Constitution's historical background will find the various writings of the founding fathers to be helpful for understanding their intentions and the reasoning behind the Constitution. The *Federalist Papers*, written by James Madison, Alexander Hamilton and John Jay to convince people in New York to ratify the Constitution, are a standard reference point. Of particular importance are also the records of the debates at the Convention in Philadelphia in 1787, mainly from Madison's notes. An even further study of constitutional law could involve examining the historical background in the English legal tradition before American independence as well as the legal history of the United States from the founding period until the present day.

To know what the laws are in the United States today, we have to look to *federal statutes*, laws passed by Congress according to the powers given it, as well as to *case law*, general rules determined in court. Being a "common law" country in the English tradition, the decisions made by courts in the United States set binding *precedents* for the future. In particular, the way that the Supreme Court has interpreted the Constitution defines how principles found in the document are implemented throughout the country. It is always possible for the Supreme Court to reverse its previous decisions and to set new precedents. By applying the rule of *equity* (fairness), it can correct or go beyond past precedents it judges to be unfair or no longer adequate. Moreover, as most laws and cases are determined at the state level, the constitutions, statutes and court decisions of the state governments are also very important. Different states may make very different laws, and states often come into conflict with the federal government about the limits of federal power (see under Article VI). Furthermore, principles in the Constitution are often (but not always) repeated in the state constitutions, but then understood in different ways, for example in applying gun laws, equal protection, and rights in the state justice systems.

In spite of the many cultural and legal differences between the various states, the Constitution focuses on the United States as a whole. It regulates the government that makes, interprets and enforces laws for the entire country and defines rights that all Americans in all states have. The framers attempted to bring diverse groups in independently-minded states together, and the amendments have continued in this spirit by defining uniform principles for the central government and for all citizens. Since the founding period, the Constitution has always been interpreted in conflicting ways, and is still appealed to by those on both sides of legal arguments. It may thus seem that the "more perfect Union" envisioned by the framers remains no more than an ideal. Nevertheless, despite all the conflicts surrounding how the Constitution should be applied in specific situations, the governmental system it establishes, the liberties and protections it guarantees, as well as its symbolic value for all Americans still continue to *unite the states.*

The future of the Constitution and the states it officially unites will continue to depend on how its principles are interpreted and applied. Demands for equal protection for people who may face different kinds of discrimination still generate controversy. As same-sex couples demand equal treatment, many who only recognize traditional marriage worry about facing discrimination themselves for their conservative beliefs. The new health care plan and attempts to legalize marijuana have raised important debates about the commerce clause and the relationship between federal and state power. Perhaps most importantly of all, the executive branch's growing power in the war on terror raises fundamental questions about how to apply the Constitution in the 21st century. On the one hand, the government insists on doing everything that it considers "necessary and proper" to protect the nation in an age of the Internet and global terror. On the other hand, some of Americans' oldest and most basic rights, those of privacy and due process guaranteed by the Fourth and Fifth Amendments, may be seriously threatened by ever-increasing government surveillance.

Further Reading

Primary Sources

Congressional Research Service, CRS Annotated Constitution (Cornell University Law School: Legal Information Institute), www.law.cornell.edu/anncon/

Farrand, Max (ed.), *The Records of the Federal Convention of 1787*, 3 volumes (Yale University Press: New Haven, 1911)

National Archives, *America's Historical Documents*, www.archives.gov/historical-docs/

Pole, Jack R. (ed.), *The American Constitution For and Against: The Federalist and the Anti-Federalist Papers* (Hill and Wang: New York, 1987)

Background / Founding Fathers

Bernstein, R. B., *The Founding Fathers Reconsidered* (Oxford University Press: Oxford et. al., 2009)

Feinberg, Barbara Silberdick, *The Articles of Confederation: The First Constitution of the United States* (Twenty-First Century Books: Hong Kong, 2002)

Ferris, Robert G. (ed.), *Signers of the Constitution: Historic Places Commemorating the Signing of the Constitution* (United States Department of the Interior, National Park Service: Washington, D.C., 1976)

Mitchell, Broadus & Louise P., *A Biography of the Constitution of the United States: Its Origin, Formation, Adoption, Interpretation* (Oxford University Press: Oxford et. al., 1975)

Pasley, Jeffrey L., et al. (ed.), *Beyond the Founding Fathers. New Approaches to the Political History of the Early American Republic* (University of North Carolina Press: Chapel Hill / London, 2004)

U.S. Government and Constitution

Black's Law Dictionary Free Online Legal Dictionary, 2nd Edition, http://thelawdictionary.org/

Clack, George (ed.), *Outline of the U.S. Legal System* (Bureau of International Information Programs, United States Department of State, 2004)

Genovese, Michael A.; Lori Cox Han (eds.), *The Presidency and the Challenge of Democracy* (Palgrave MacMillan: New York, 2006)

Rehnquist, William H., *The Supreme Court* (Vintage Books: New York, 2001)

Smith, Steven S. et al., *The American Congress* (Cambridge University Press: Cambridge et al., 2011)

Tribe, Laurence, *Constitutional Law*, 3rd Edition, (Foundation Press: New York, 2000)

The Bill of Rights and Other Amendments

Bernstein, Richard B., "The Sleeper Wakes: The History and Legacy of the Twenty-Seventh Amendment," *Fordham Law Review*, Volume 61, Issue 3, pp. 497-557 (1992)

Byrd, B. Sharon, *Introduction to Anglo-American Law & Language*, 2nd edition (C.H. Beck: Munich, 2000)

Cullen-DuPont, Kathryn, *Encyclopedia of Women's History in America*, 2nd edition (Facts on File: New York, 2000)

Davis, Derek H. (ed.), *The Oxford Handbook of Church and State in the United States* (Oxford University Press: Oxford et. al., 2010)

Lambert, Frank, *The Founding Fathers and The Place of Religion in America* (Princeton University Press: Princeton, NJ, 2003)

Marion, Nancy E., *Federal Government and Criminal Justice* (Palgrave MacMillian: New York, 2011)

Vorenberg, Michael, *Final Freedom: The Civil War, the Abolition of Slavery, and the Thirteenth Amendment* (Cambridge University Press: Cambridge et. al., 2001)

Zacharias, Gary & Jared (eds.), *The Bill of Rights* (Greenhaven Press: San Diego et. al., 2003)

Appendix A: The Constitution of the United States of America

Articles I-VII
[Proposed 1787; Ratified 1789]

Preamble

We the People of the United States, in Order to form a more perfect Union, establish Justice, insure domestic Tranquility, provide for the common defence, promote the general Welfare, and secure the Blessings of Liberty to ourselves and our Posterity, do ordain and establish this Constitution for the United States of America.

Article I.

Section. 1. All legislative Powers herein granted shall be vested in a Congress of the United States, which shall consist of a Senate and House of Representatives.

Section. 2. The House of Representatives shall be composed of Members chosen every second Year by the People of the several States, and the Electors in each State shall have the Qualifications requisite for Electors of the most numerous Branch of the State Legislature.

No Person shall be a Representative who shall not have attained to the Age of twenty five Years, and been seven Years a Citizen of the United States, and who shall not, when elected, be an Inhabitant of that State in which he shall be chosen.

Representatives and direct Taxes shall be apportioned among the several States which may be included within this Union, according to their respective Numbers, *which shall be determined by adding to the whole Number of free Persons, including those bound to Service for a Term of Years, and excluding Indians not taxed, three fifths of all other Persons [Modified by Amendments XIII and*

XIV]. The actual Enumeration shall be made within three Years after the first Meeting of the Congress of the United States, and within every subsequent Term of ten Years, in such Manner as they shall by Law direct. The Number of Representatives shall not exceed one for every thirty Thousand, but each State shall have at Least one Representative; and until such enumeration shall be made, the State of New Hampshire shall be entitled to chuse three, Massachusetts eight, Rhode-Island and Providence Plantations one, Connecticut five, New-York six, New Jersey four, Pennsylvania eight, Delaware one, Maryland six, Virginia ten, North Carolina five, South Carolina five, and Georgia three.

When vacancies happen in the Representation from any State, the Executive Authority thereof shall issue Writs of Election to fill such Vacancies.

The House of Representatives shall chuse their Speaker and other Officers; and shall have the sole Power of Impeachment.

Section. 3. The Senate of the United States shall be composed of two Senators from each State, *chosen by the Legislature thereof* [*Modified by Amendment XVII*] for six Years; and each Senator shall have one Vote.

Immediately after they shall be assembled in Consequence of the first Election, they shall be divided as equally as may be into three Classes. The Seats of the Senators of the first Class shall be vacated at the Expiration of the second Year, of the second Class at the Expiration of the fourth Year, and of the third Class at the Expiration of the sixth Year, so that one third may be chosen every second Year; *and if Vacancies happen by Resignation, or otherwise, during the Recess of the Legislature of any State, the Executive thereof may make temporary Appointments until the next Meeting of the Legislature, which shall then fill such Vacancies* [*Modified by Amendment XVII*].

No Person shall be a Senator who shall not have attained to the Age of thirty Years, and been nine Years a Citizen of the United States, and who shall not, when elected, be an Inhabitant of that State for which he shall be chosen.

The Vice President of the United States shall be President of the Senate, but shall have no Vote, unless they be equally divided.

The Senate shall chuse their other Officers, and also a President pro tempore, in the Absence of the Vice President, or when he shall exercise the Office of President of the United States.

The Senate shall have the sole Power to try all Impeachments. When sitting for that Purpose, they shall be on Oath or Affirmation. When the President of the United States is tried, the Chief Justice shall preside: And no Person shall be convicted without the Concurrence of two thirds of the Members present.

Judgment in Cases of Impeachment shall not extend further than to removal from Office, and disqualification to hold and enjoy any Office of honor, Trust or Profit under the United States: but the Party convicted shall nevertheless be liable and subject to Indictment, Trial, Judgment and Punishment, according to Law.

Section. 4. The Times, Places and Manner of holding Elections for Senators and Representatives, shall be prescribed in each State by the Legislature thereof; but the Congress may at any time by Law make or alter such Regulations, except as to the Places of chusing Senators.

The Congress shall assemble at least once in every Year, and such Meeting shall be *on the first Monday in December* [*Modified by Amendment XX*], unless they shall by Law appoint a different Day.

Section. 5. Each House shall be the Judge of the Elections, Returns and Qualifications of its own Members, and a Majority of each shall constitute a Quorum to do Business; but a smaller Number may adjourn from day to day, and may be authorized to compel the Attendance of absent Members, in such Manner, and under such Penalties as each House may provide.

Each House may determine the Rules of its Proceedings, punish its Members for disorderly Behaviour, and, with the Concurrence of two thirds, expel a Member.

Each House shall keep a Journal of its Proceedings, and from time to time publish the same, excepting such Parts as may in their Judgment require Secrecy; and the Yeas and Nays of the Members of either House on any question shall, at the Desire of one fifth of those Present, be entered on the Journal.

Neither House, during the Session of Congress, shall, without the Consent of the other, adjourn for more than three days, nor to any other Place than that in which the two Houses shall be sitting.

Section. 6. The Senators and Representatives shall receive a Compensation for their Services, to be ascertained by Law, and paid out of the Treasury of the United States. They shall in all Cases, except Treason, Felony and Breach of the Peace, be privileged from Arrest during their Attendance at the Session of their respective Houses, and in going to and returning from the same; and for any Speech or Debate in either House, they shall not be questioned in any other Place.

No Senator or Representative shall, during the Time for which he was elected, be appointed to any civil Office under the Authority of the United States, which shall have been created, or the Emoluments whereof shall have been encreased during such time; and no Person holding any Office under the United States, shall be a Member of either House during his Continuance in Office.

Section. 7. All Bills for raising Revenue shall originate in the House of Representatives; but the Senate may propose or concur with Amendments as on other Bills.

Every Bill which shall have passed the House of Representatives and the Senate, shall, before it become a Law, be presented to the President of the United States: If he approve he shall sign it, but if not he shall return it, with his Objections to that House in which it shall have originated, who shall enter the Objections at large on their Journal, and proceed to reconsider it. If after such Reconsideration two thirds of that House shall agree to pass the Bill, it shall be sent, together with the Objections, to the other House, by which it shall likewise be reconsidered, and if approved by two thirds of that House, it shall become a Law. But in all such Cases the Votes of both Houses shall be determined by yeas and Nays, and the Names of the Persons voting for and against the Bill shall be entered on the Journal of each House respectively. If any Bill shall not be returned by the President within ten Days (Sundays excepted) after it shall have been presented to him, the Same shall be a Law, in like Manner as if he had signed it, unless the Congress by their Adjournment prevent its Return, in which Case it shall not be a Law.

Every Order, Resolution, or Vote to which the Concurrence of the Senate and House of Representatives may be necessary (except on a question of Adjournment) shall be presented to the President of the United States; and before the Same shall take Effect, shall be approved by him, or being disapproved by him, shall be repassed by two thirds of the Senate and House of Representatives, according to the Rules and Limitations prescribed in the Case of a Bill.

Section. 8. The Congress shall have Power To lay and collect Taxes, Duties, Imposts and Excises, to pay the Debts and provide for the common Defence and general Welfare of the United States; but all Duties, Imposts and Excises shall be uniform throughout the United States;

To borrow Money on the credit of the United States;

To regulate Commerce with foreign Nations, and among the several States, and with the Indian Tribes;

To establish an uniform Rule of Naturalization, and uniform Laws on the subject of Bankruptcies throughout the United States;

To coin Money, regulate the Value thereof, and of foreign Coin, and fix the Standard of Weights and Measures;

To provide for the Punishment of counterfeiting the Securities and current Coin of the United States;

To establish Post Offices and post Roads;

To promote the Progress of Science and useful Arts, by securing for limited Times to Authors and Inventors the exclusive Right to their respective Writings and Discoveries;

To constitute Tribunals inferior to the supreme Court;

To define and punish Piracies and Felonies committed on the high Seas, and Offences against the Law of Nations;

To declare War, grant Letters of Marque and Reprisal, and make Rules concerning Captures on Land and Water;

To raise and support Armies, but no Appropriation of Money to that Use shall be for a longer Term than two Years;

To provide and maintain a Navy;

To make Rules for the Government and Regulation of the land and naval Forces;

To provide for calling forth the Militia to execute the Laws of the Union, suppress Insurrections and repel Invasions;

To provide for organizing, arming, and disciplining, the Militia, and for governing such Part of them as may be employed in the Service of the United States, reserving to the States respectively, the Appointment of the Officers, and the Authority of training the Militia according to the discipline prescribed by Congress;

To exercise exclusive Legislation in all Cases whatsoever, over such District (not exceeding ten Miles square) as may, by Cession of particular States, and the Acceptance of Congress, become the Seat of the Government of the United States, and to exercise like Authority over all Places purchased by the Consent of the Legislature of the State in which the Same shall be, for the Erection of Forts, Magazines, Arsenals, dock-Yards, and other needful Buildings; – And

To make all Laws which shall be necessary and proper for carrying into Execution the foregoing Powers, and all other Powers vested by this Constitution in the Government of the United States, or in any Department or Officer thereof.

Section. 9. The Migration or Importation of such Persons as any of the States now existing shall think proper to admit, shall not be prohibited by the Congress prior to the Year one thousand eight hundred and eight, but a Tax or duty may be imposed on such Importation, not exceeding ten dollars for each Person.

The Privilege of the Writ of Habeas Corpus shall not be suspended, unless when in Cases of Rebellion or Invasion the public Safety may require it.

No Bill of Attainder or ex post facto Law shall be passed.

No Capitation, or other direct, Tax shall be laid, *unless in Proportion to the Census or enumeration herein before directed to be taken [Modlified by Amendment XVI].*

No Tax or Duty shall be laid on Articles exported from any State.

No Preference shall be given by any Regulation of Commerce or Revenue to the Ports of one State over those of another; nor shall Vessels bound to, or from, one State, be obliged to enter, clear, or pay Duties in another.

No Money shall be drawn from the Treasury, but in Consequence of Appropriations made by Law; and a regular Statement and Account of the Receipts and Expenditures of all public Money shall be published from time to time.

No Title of Nobility shall be granted by the United States: And no Person holding any Office of Profit or Trust under them, shall, without the Consent of the Congress, accept of any present, Emolument, Office, or Title, of any kind whatever, from any King, Prince, or foreign State.

Section. 10. No State shall enter into any Treaty, Alliance, or Confederation; grant Letters of Marque and Reprisal; coin Money; emit Bills of Credit; make any Thing but gold and silver Coin a Tender in Payment of Debts; pass any Bill of Attainder, ex post facto Law, or Law impairing the Obligation of Contracts, or grant any Title of Nobility.

No State shall, without the Consent of the Congress, lay any Imposts or Duties on Imports or Exports, except what may be absolutely necessary for executing it's inspection Laws: and the net Produce of all Duties and Imposts, laid by any State on Imports or Exports, shall be for the Use of the Treasury of the United States; and all such Laws shall be subject to the Revision and Controul of the Congress.

No State shall, without the Consent of Congress, lay any Duty of Tonnage, keep Troops, or Ships of War in time of Peace, enter into any Agreement or Compact with another State, or with a foreign Power, or engage in War, unless actually invaded, or in such imminent Danger as will not admit of delay.

Article II.

Section. 1. The executive Power shall be vested in a President of the United States of America. He shall hold his Office during the Term of four Years, and, together with the Vice President, chosen for the same Term, be elected, as follows:

Each State shall appoint, in such Manner as the Legislature thereof may direct, a Number of Electors, equal to the whole Number of Senators and Representatives to which the State may be entitled in the Congress: but no Senator or Representative, or Person holding an Office of Trust or Profit under the United States, shall be appointed an Elector.

The Electors shall meet in their respective States, and vote by Ballot for two Persons, of whom one at least shall not be an Inhabitant of the same State with themselves. And they shall make a List of all the Persons voted for, and of the Number of Votes for each; which List they shall sign and certify, and transmit sealed to the Seat of the Government of the United States, directed to the President of the Senate. The President of the Senate shall, in the Presence of the Senate and House of Representatives, open all the Certificates, and the Votes shall then be counted. The Person having the greatest Number of Votes shall be the President, if such Number be a Majority of the whole Number of Electors appointed; and if there be more than one who have such Majority, and have an equal Number of Votes, then the House of Representatives shall immediately chuse by Ballot one of them for President; and if no Person have a Majority, then from the five highest on the List the said House shall in like Manner chuse the President. But in chusing the President, the Votes shall be taken by States, the Representation from each State having one Vote; A quorum for this purpose shall consist of a Member or Members from two thirds of the States, and a Majority of all the States shall be necessary to a Choice. In every Case, after the Choice of the President, the Person having the greatest Number of Votes of the Electors shall be the Vice President. But if there should remain two or more who have equal Votes, the Senate shall chuse from them by Ballot the Vice President. [Modified by Amendment XII]

The Congress may determine the Time of chusing the Electors, and the Day on which they shall give their Votes; which Day shall be the same throughout the United States.

No Person except a natural born Citizen, or a Citizen of the United States, at the time of the Adoption of this Constitution, shall be eligible to the Office of President; neither shall any Person be eligible to that Office who shall not have attained to the Age of thirty five Years, and been fourteen Years a Resident within the United States.

In Case of the Removal of the President from Office, or of his Death, Resignation, or Inability to discharge the Powers and Duties of the said Office, the Same shall devolve on the Vice President, and the Congress may by Law provide for the Case of Removal, Death, Resignation or Inability, both of the President and Vice President, declaring what Officer shall then act as President, and such Officer shall act accordingly, until the Disability be removed, or a President shall be elected. [Modified by Amendment XXV]

The President shall, at stated Times, receive for his Services, a Compensation, which shall neither be increased nor diminished during the Period for which he shall have been elected, and he shall not receive within that Period any other Emolument from the United States, or any of them.

Before he enter on the Execution of his Office, he shall take the following Oath or Affirmation: – "I do solemnly swear (or affirm) that I will faithfully execute the Office of President of the United States, and will to the best of my Ability, preserve, protect and defend the Constitution of the United States."

Section. 2. The President shall be Commander in Chief of the Army and Navy of the United States, and of the Militia of the several States, when called into the actual Service of the United States; he may require the Opinion, in writing, of the principal Officer in each of the executive Departments, upon any Subject relating to the Duties of their respective Offices, and he shall have Power to grant Reprieves and Pardons for Offences against the United States, except in Cases of Impeachment.

He shall have Power, by and with the Advice and Consent of the Senate, to make Treaties, provided two thirds of the Senators present concur; and he shall nominate, and by and with the Advice and Consent of the Senate, shall appoint Ambassadors, other public Ministers and Consuls, Judges of the supreme Court, and all other Officers of the United States, whose Appointments are not herein otherwise provided for, and which shall be established by Law: but the Congress may by Law vest the Appointment of such inferior Officers, as they think proper, in the President alone, in the Courts of Law, or in the Heads of Departments.

The President shall have Power to fill up all Vacancies that may happen during the Recess of the Senate, by granting Commissions which shall expire at the End of their next Session.

Section. 3. He shall from time to time give to the Congress Information of the State of the Union, and recommend to their Consideration such Measures as he shall judge necessary and expedient; he may, on extraordinary Occasions, convene both Houses, or either of them, and in Case of Disagreement between them, with Respect to the Time of

Adjournment, he may adjourn them to such Time as he shall think proper; he shall receive Ambassadors and other public Ministers; he shall take Care that the Laws be faithfully executed, and shall Commission all the Officers of the United States.

Section. 4. The President, Vice President and all civil Officers of the United States, shall be removed from Office on Impeachment for, and Conviction of, Treason, Bribery, or other high Crimes and Misdemeanors.

Article III.

Section. 1. The judicial Power of the United States shall be vested in one supreme Court, and in such inferior Courts as the Congress may from time to time ordain and establish. The Judges, both of the supreme and inferior Courts, shall hold their Offices during good Behaviour, and shall, at stated Times, receive for their Services a Compensation, which shall not be diminished during their Continuance in Office.

Section. 2. The judicial Power shall extend to all Cases, in Law and Equity, arising under this Constitution, the Laws of the United States, and Treaties made, or which shall be made, under their Authority; – to all Cases affecting Ambassadors, other public Ministers and Consuls; – to all Cases of admiralty and maritime Jurisdiction; – to Controversies to which the United States shall be a Party; – to Controversies between two or more States; – *between a State and Citizens of another State [Nullified by Amendment XI]*, – between Citizens of different States, – between Citizens of the same State claiming Lands under Grants of different States, and between a State, or the Citizens thereof, and foreign States, Citizens or Subjects.

In all Cases affecting Ambassadors, other public Ministers and Consuls, and those in which a State shall be Party, the supreme Court shall have original Jurisdiction. In all the other Cases before mentioned, the supreme Court shall have appellate Jurisdiction, both as to Law and Fact, with such Exceptions, and under such Regulations as the Congress shall make.

The Trial of all Crimes, except in Cases of Impeachment, shall be by Jury; and such Trial shall be held in the State where the said Crimes shall have been committed; but when not committed within any State, the Trial shall be at such Place or Places as the Congress may by Law have directed.

Section. 3. Treason against the United States, shall consist only in levying War against them, or in adhering to their Enemies, giving them Aid and Comfort. No Person shall be convicted of Treason unless on the Testimony of two Witnesses to the same overt Act, or on Confession in open Court.

The Congress shall have Power to declare the Punishment of Treason, but no Attainder of Treason shall work Corruption of Blood, or Forfeiture except during the Life of the Person attainted.

Article IV.

Section 1. Full Faith and Credit shall be given in each State to the public Acts, Records, and judicial Proceedings of every other State. And the Congress may by general Laws prescribe the Manner in which such Acts, Records and Proceedings shall be proved, and the Effect thereof.

Section 2. The Citizens of each State shall be entitled to all Privileges and Immunities of Citizens in the several States.

A Person charged in any State with Treason, Felony, or other Crime, who shall flee from Justice, and be found in another State, shall on Demand of the executive Authority of the State from which he fled, be delivered up, to be removed to the State having Jurisdiction of the Crime.

No Person held to Service or Labour in one State, under the Laws thereof, escaping into another, shall, in Consequence of any Law or Regulation therein, be discharged from such Service or Labour, but shall be delivered up on Claim of the Party to whom such Service or Labour may be due [Nullified by Amendment XIII].

Section 3. New States may be admitted by the Congress into this Union; but no new State shall be formed or erected within the Jurisdiction of any other State; nor any State be formed by the Junction of two or more States, or Parts of States, without the Consent of the Legislatures of the States concerned as well as of the Congress.

The Congress shall have Power to dispose of and make all needful Rules and Regulations respecting the Territory or other Property belonging to the United States; and nothing in this Constitution shall be so construed as to Prejudice any Claims of the United States, or of any particular State.

Section 4. The United States shall guarantee to every State in this Union a Republican Form of Government, and shall protect each of them against Invasion; and on Application of the Legislature, or of the Executive (when the Legislature cannot be convened), against domestic Violence.

Article V.

The Congress, whenever two thirds of both Houses shall deem it necessary, shall propose Amendments to this Constitution, or, on the Application of the Legislatures of two thirds of the several States, shall call a Convention for proposing Amendments, which, in either Case, shall be valid to all Intents and Purposes, as Part of this Constitution, when ratified by the Legislatures of three fourths of the several States, or by Conventions in three fourths thereof, as the one or the other Mode of Ratification may be proposed by the Congress; Provided that no Amendment which may be made prior to the Year One thousand eight hundred and eight shall in any Manner affect the first and fourth Clauses in the Ninth Section of the first Article; and that no State, without its Consent, shall be deprived of its equal Suffrage in the Senate.

Article VI.

All Debts contracted and Engagements entered into, before the Adoption of this Constitution, shall be as valid against the United States under this Constitution, as under the Confederation.

This Constitution, and the Laws of the United States which shall be made in Pursuance thereof; and all Treaties made, or which shall be made, under the Authority of the United States, shall be the supreme Law of the Land; and the Judges in every State shall be bound thereby, any Thing in the Constitution or Laws of any State to the Contrary notwithstanding.

The Senators and Representatives before mentioned, and the Members of the several State Legislatures, and all executive and judicial Officers, both of the United States and of the several States, shall be bound by Oath or Affirmation, to support this Constitution; but no religious Test shall ever be required as a Qualification to any Office or public Trust under the United States.

Article VII.

The Ratification of the Conventions of nine States, shall be sufficient for the Establishment of this Constitution between the States so ratifying the Same.

The Word, "the," being interlined between the seventh and eighth Lines of the first Page, the Word "Thirty" being partly written on an Erazure in the fifteenth Line of the first Page, The Words "is tried" being interlined between the thirty second and thirty third Lines of the first Page and the Word "the" being interlined between the forty third and forty fourth Lines of the second Page.

Attest William Jackson Secretary

done in Convention by the Unanimous Consent of the States present the Seventeenth Day of September in the Year of our Lord one thousand seven hundred and Eighty seven and of the Independance of the United States of America the Twelfth In witness whereof We have hereunto subscribed our Names,

Go. Washington – Presidt.
W. Jackson Secretary

Delaware
Geo: Read
Gunning Bedford jun
John Dickinson
Richard Bassett
Jaco: Broom

Maryland
James McHenry
Dan of St Thos. Jenifer
Danl. Carroll

Virginia
John Blair
James Madison Jr.

North Carolina
Wm. Blount
Richd. Dobbs Spaight
Hu Williamson

South Carolina
J. Rutledge
Charles Cotesworth Pinckney
Charles Pinckney
Pierce Butler

Georgia
William Few
Abr Baldwin

New Hampshire
John Langdon
Nicholas Gilman

Massachusetts
Nathaniel Gorham
Rufus King

Connecticut
Wm. Saml. Johnson
Roger Sherman

New York
Alexander Hamilton

New Jersey
Wil: Livingston
David Brearly
Wm. Paterson
Jona: Dayton

Pennsylvania
B Franklin
Thomas Mifflin
Robt. Morris
Geo. Clymer
Thos. FitzSimons
Jared Ingersoll
James Wilson
Gouv Morris

In Convention, Monday, September 17th. 1787

Present
The States of
New Hampshire, Massachusetts, Connecticut, Mr. Hamilton from New York, New Jersey, Pennsylvania, Delaware, Maryland, Virginia, North Carolina, South Carolina and Georgia.

RESOLVED, That the preceding Constitution be laid before the united States in Congress assembled, and that it is the opinion of this Convention, that it afterwards be submitted to a Convention of Delegates, chosen in each State by the People thereof, under the Recommendation of its Legislature, for their Assent and Ratification; and that such Convention assenting to, and verifying the Same, should give Notice thereof, to the United States in Congress assembled.

RESOLVED, That it is the Opinion of this Convention, that as soon as the Conventions of nine States shall have ratified this Constitution, the United States in Congress assembled should fix a Day on which Electors shall be appointed by the States which shall have ratified the same, and a day on which the Electors should assemble to vote for the President, and the Time and Place for commencing Proceedings under this Constitution. That after such Publication the Electors should be appointed, and the Senators and Representatives elected. That the Electors should meet on the Day fixed for the Election of the President, and should transmit these Votes, certified, signed, sealed, and delivered, as the Constitution requires, to the Secretary of the United States in Congress assembled, that the Senators and Representatives should convene at the Time and Place assigned; that the Senators should appoint a President of the Senate, for the end Purpose of receiving, opening and counting the Votes for President; and after he shall be chosen, the Congress, together with the President, should, without Delay, proceed to execute this Constitution.

By the Unanimous Order of the Convention

Go. Washington – Presidt.
W. Jackson Secretary

The Bill of Rights
[Proposed 1789; Ratified 1791]

Congress of the United States begun and held at the City of New-York, on Wednesday the fourth of March, one thousand seven hundred and eighty nine.

THE Conventions of a number of the States, having at the time of their adopting the Constitution, expressed a desire, in order to prevent misconstruction or abuse of its powers, that further declaratory and restrictive clauses should be added: And as extending the ground of public confidence in the Government, will best ensure the beneficent ends of its institution.

RESOLVED by the Senate and House of Representatives of the United States of America, in Congress assembled, two thirds of both Houses concurring, that the following Articles be proposed to the Legislatures of the several States, as amendments to the Constitution of the United States, all, or any of which Articles, when ratified by three fourths of the said Legislatures, to be valid to all intents and purposes, as part of the said Constitution; viz.

ARTICLES in addition to, and Amendment of the Constitution of the United States of America, proposed by Congress, and ratified by the Legislatures of the several States, pursuant to the fifth Article of the original Constitution.

Amendment I.

Congress shall make no law respecting an establishment of religion, or prohibiting the free exercise thereof; or abridging the freedom of speech, or of the press; or the right of the people peaceably to assemble, and to petition the Government for a redress of grievances.

Amendment II.

A well regulated Militia, being necessary to the security of a free State, the right of the people to keep and bear Arms, shall not be infringed.

Amendment III.

No Soldier shall, in time of peace be quartered in any house, without the consent of the Owner, nor in time of war, but in a manner to be prescribed by law.

Amendment IV.

The right of the people to be secure in their persons, houses, papers, and effects, against unreasonable searches and seizures, shall not be violated, and no Warrants shall issue, but upon probable cause, supported by Oath or affirmation, and particularly describing the place to be searched, and the persons or things to be seized.

Amendment V.

No person shall be held to answer for a capital, or otherwise infamous crime, unless on a presentment or indictment of a Grand Jury, except in cases arising in the land or naval forces, or in the Militia, when in actual service in time of War or public danger; nor shall any person be subject for the same offence to be twice put in jeopardy of life or limb; nor shall be compelled in any criminal case to be a witness against himself, nor be deprived of life, liberty, or property, without due process of law; nor shall private property be taken for public use, without just compensation.

Amendment VI.

In all criminal prosecutions, the accused shall enjoy the right to a speedy and public trial, by an impartial jury of the State and district wherein the crime shall have been committed, which district shall have been previously ascertained by law, and to be informed of the nature and cause of the accusation; to be confronted with the witnesses against him; to have compulsory process for obtaining witnesses in his favor, and to have the Assistance of Counsel for his defense.

Amendment VII.

In Suits at common law, where the value in controversy shall exceed twenty dollars, the right of trial by jury shall be preserved, and no fact tried by a jury, shall be otherwise re-examined in any Court of the United States, than according to the rules of the common law.

Amendment VIII.

Excessive bail shall not be required, nor excessive fines imposed, nor cruel and unusual punishments inflicted.

Amendment IX.

The enumeration in the Constitution, of certain rights, shall not be construed to deny or disparage others retained by the people.

Amendment X.

The powers not delegated to the United States by the Constitution, nor prohibited by it to the States, are reserved to the States respectively, or to the people.

Additional Amendments to the Constitution

Amendment XI.
[Proposed 1794; Ratified 1795]

The Judicial power of the United States shall not be construed to extend to any suit in law or equity, commenced or prosecuted against one of the United States by Citizens of another State, or by Citizens or Subjects of any Foreign State.

Amendment XII.
[Proposed 1803; Ratified 1804]

The Electors shall meet in their respective states and vote by ballot for President and Vice-President, one of whom, at least, shall not be an inhabitant of the same state with themselves; they shall name in their ballots the person voted for as President, and in distinct ballots the person voted for as Vice-President, and they shall make distinct lists of all persons voted for as President, and of all persons voted for as Vice-President, and of the number of votes for each, which lists they shall sign and certify, and transmit sealed to the seat of the government of the United States, directed to the President of the Senate; – the President of the Senate shall, in the presence of the Senate and House of Representatives, open all the certificates and the votes shall then be counted; – The person having the greatest number of votes for President, shall be the President, if such number be a majority of the whole number of Electors appointed; and if no person have such majority, then from the persons having the highest numbers not exceeding three on the list of those voted for as President, the House of Representatives shall choose immediately, by ballot, the President. But in choosing the President, the votes shall be taken by states, the representation from each state having one vote; a quorum for this purpose shall consist of a member or members from two-thirds of the states, and a majority of all the states shall be necessary to a choice. *And if the House of Representatives shall not choose a President whenever the right of choice shall devolve upon them, before the fourth day of March next following, then the Vice-President shall act as President, as in case of the death or other constitutional disability of the President* [*Modified by Amendment XX, Section 3*]. The person having the greatest number of votes as Vice-President, shall be the Vice-President, if such number be a majority of the whole number of Electors appointed, and if no person have a majority, then from the two highest numbers on the list, the Senate shall choose the Vice-President; a quorum for the purpose shall consist of two-thirds of the whole number of Senators, and a majority of the whole number shall be necessary to a choice. But no person constitutionally ineligible to the office of President shall be eligible to that of Vice-President of the United States.

Amendment XIII.
[Proposed 1865; Ratified 1865]

Section 1. Neither slavery nor involuntary servitude, except as a punishment for crime whereof the party shall have been duly convicted, shall exist within the United States, or any place subject to their jurisdiction.

Section 2. Congress shall have power to enforce this article by appropriate legislation.

Amendment XIV.
[Proposed 1866; Ratified 1868]

Section 1. All persons born or naturalized in the United States, and subject to the jurisdiction thereof, are citizens of the United States and of the State wherein they reside. No State shall make or enforce any law which shall abridge the privileges or immunities of citizens of the United States; nor shall any State deprive any person of life, liberty, or property, without due process of law; nor deny to any person within its jurisdiction the equal protection of the laws.

Section 2. Representatives shall be apportioned among the several States according to their respective numbers, counting the whole number of persons in each State, excluding Indians not taxed. But when the right to vote at any election for the choice of electors for President and Vice-President of the United States, Representatives in Congress, the Executive and Judicial officers of a State, or the members of the Legislature thereof, is denied to any of the male inhabitants of such State, being twenty-one years of age, and citizens of the United States, or in any way abridged, except for participation in rebellion, or other crime, the basis of representation therein shall be reduced in the proportion which the number of such male citizens shall bear to the whole number of male citizens twenty-one years of age in such State.

Section 3. No person shall be a Senator or Representative in Congress, or elector of President and Vice-President, or hold any office, civil or military, under the United States, or under any State, who, having previously taken an oath, as a member of Congress, or as an officer of the United States, or as a member of any State legislature, or as an executive or judicial officer of any State, to support the Constitution of the United States, shall have engaged in insurrection or rebellion against the same, or given aid or comfort to the enemies thereof. But Congress may by a vote of two-thirds of each House, remove such disability.

Section 4. The validity of the public debt of the United States, authorized by law, including debts incurred for payment of pensions and bounties for services in suppressing insurrection or rebellion, shall not be questioned. But neither the United States nor any State shall assume or pay any debt or obligation incurred in aid of insurrection or rebellion against the United States, or any claim for the loss or emancipation of any slave; but all such debts, obligations and claims shall be held illegal and void.

Section 5. The Congress shall have the power to enforce, by appropriate legislation, the provisions of this article.

Amendment XV.
[Proposed 1869; Ratified 1870]

Section 1. The right of citizens of the United States to vote shall not be denied or abridged by the United States or by any State on account of race, color, or previous condition of servitude –

Section 2. The Congress shall have the power to enforce this article by appropriate legislation.

Amendment XVI.
[Proposed 1909; Ratified 1913]

The Congress shall have power to lay and collect taxes on incomes, from whatever source derived, without apportionment among the several States, and without regard to any census or enumeration.

Amendment XVII.
[Proposed 1912; Ratified 1913]

The Senate of the United States shall be composed of two Senators from each State, elected by the people thereof, for six years; and each Senator shall have one vote. The electors in each State shall have the qualifications requisite for electors of the most numerous branch of the State legislatures.

When vacancies happen in the representation of any State in the Senate, the executive authority of such State shall issue writs of election to fill such vacancies: *Provided*, That the legislature of any State may empower the executive thereof to make temporary appointments until the people fill the vacancies by election as the legislature may direct.

This amendment shall not be so construed as to affect the election or term of any Senator chosen before it becomes valid as part of the Constitution.

Amendment XVIII.
[Proposed 1917; Ratified 1919; Repealed 1933]

Section 1. After one year from the ratification of this article the manufacture, sale, or transportation of intoxicating liquors within, the importation thereof into, or the exportation thereof from the United States and all territory subject to the jurisdiction thereof for beverage purposes is hereby prohibited.

Section 2. The Congress and the several States shall have concurrent power to enforce this article by appropriate legislation.

Section 3. This article shall be inoperative unless it shall have been ratified as an amendment to the Constitution by the legislatures of the several

States, as provided in the Constitution, within seven years from the date of the submission hereof to the States by the Congress.

Amendment XIX.
[Proposed 1919; Ratified 1920]

The right of citizens of the United States to vote shall not be denied or abridged by the United States or by any State on account of sex.

Congress shall have power to enforce this article by appropriate legislation.

Amendment XX.
[Proposed 1932; Ratified 1933]

Section 1. The terms of the President and the Vice President shall end at noon on the 20th day of January, and the terms of Senators and Representatives at noon on the 3rd day of January, of the years in which such terms would have ended if this article had not been ratified; and the terms of their successors shall then begin.

Section 2. The Congress shall assemble at least once in every year, and such meeting shall begin at noon on the 3d day of January, unless they shall by law appoint a different day.

Section 3. If, at the time fixed for the beginning of the term of the President, the President elect shall have died, the Vice President elect shall become President. If a President shall not have been chosen before the time fixed for the beginning of his term, or if the President elect shall have failed to qualify, then the Vice President elect shall act as President until a President shall have qualified; and the Congress may by law provide for the case wherein neither a President elect nor a Vice President shall have qualified, declaring who shall then act as President, or the manner in which one who is to act shall be selected, and such person shall act accordingly until a President or Vice President shall have qualified.

Section 4. The Congress may by law provide for the case of the death of any of the persons from whom the House of Representatives may choose a President whenever the right of choice shall have devolved upon them, and for the case of the death of any of the persons from whom the Senate may choose a Vice President whenever the right of choice shall have devolved upon them.

Section 5. Sections 1 and 2 shall take effect on the 15th day of October following the ratification of this article.

Section 6. This article shall be inoperative unless it shall have been ratified as an amendment to the Constitution by the legislatures of three-fourths of the several States within seven years from the date of its submission.

Amendment XXI.
[Proposed 1933; Ratified 1933]

Section 1. The eighteenth article of amendment to the Constitution of the United States is hereby repealed.

Section 2. The transportation or importation into any State, Territory, or Possession of the United States for delivery or use therein of intoxicating liquors, in violation of the laws thereof, is hereby prohibited.

Section 3. This article shall be inoperative unless it shall have been ratified as an amendment to the Constitution by conventions in the several States, as provided in the Constitution, within seven years from the date of the submission hereof to the States by the Congress.

Amendment XXII.
[Proposed 1947; Ratified 1951]

Section 1. No person shall be elected to the office of the President more than twice, and no person who has held the office of President, or acted as President, for more than two years of a term to which some other person was elected President shall be elected to the office of President more than once. But this Article shall not apply to any person holding the office of President when this Article was proposed by Congress, and shall not prevent any person who may be holding the office of President, or acting as President, during the term within which this Article becomes operative from holding the office of President or acting as President during the remainder of such term.

Section 2. This article shall be inoperative unless it shall have been ratified as an amendment to the Constitution by the legislatures of three-fourths of the several States within seven years from the date of its submission to the States by the Congress.

Amendment XXIII.
[Proposed 1960; Ratified 1961]

Section 1. The District constituting the seat of Government of the United States shall appoint in such manner as Congress may direct:

A number of electors of President and Vice President equal to the whole number of Senators and Representatives in Congress to which the District would be entitled if it were a State, but in no event more than the least populous State; they shall be in addition to those appointed by the States, but they shall be considered, for the purposes of the election of President and Vice President, to be electors appointed by a State; and they shall meet in the District and perform such duties as provided by the twelfth article of amendment.

Section 2. The Congress shall have power to enforce this article by appropriate legislation.

Amendment XXIV.
[Proposed 1962; Ratified 1964]

Section 1. The right of citizens of the United States to vote in any primary or other election for President or Vice President, for electors for President or Vice President, or for Senator or Representative in Congress, shall not be denied or abridged by the United States or any State by reason of failure to pay poll tax or other tax.

Section 2. The Congress shall have power to enforce this article by appropriate legislation.

Amendment XXV.
[Proposed 1965; Ratified 1967]

Section 1. In case of the removal of the President from office or of his death or resignation, the Vice President shall become President.

Section 2. Whenever there is a vacancy in the office of the Vice President, the President shall nominate a Vice President who shall take office upon confirmation by a majority vote of both Houses of Congress.

Section 3. Whenever the President transmits to the President pro tempore of the Senate and the Speaker of the House of Representatives his written declaration that he is unable to discharge the powers and duties of his office, and until he transmits to them a written declaration to the contrary, such powers and duties shall be discharged by the Vice President as Acting President.

Section 4. Whenever the Vice President and a majority of either the principal officers of the executive departments or of such other body as Congress may by law provide, transmit to the President pro tempore of the Senate and the Speaker of the House of Representatives their written declaration that the President is unable to discharge the powers and duties of his office, the Vice President shall immediately assume the powers and duties of the office as Acting President.

Thereafter, when the President transmits to the President pro tempore of the Senate and the Speaker of the House of Representatives his written declaration that no inability exists, he shall resume the powers and duties of his office unless the Vice President and a majority of either the principal officers of the executive department or of such other body as Congress may by law provide, transmit within four days to the President pro tempore of the Senate and the Speaker of the House of Representatives their written declaration that the President is unable to discharge the powers and duties of his office. Thereupon Congress shall decide the issue, assembling within forty-eight hours for that purpose if not in session. If the Congress, within twenty-one days after receipt of the latter written declaration, or, if Congress is not in session, within twenty-one days after Congress is required to assemble, determines by two-thirds vote of both Houses that the President is unable to discharge the powers and duties of his office, the Vice President shall continue to discharge the same as Acting

President; otherwise, the President shall resume the powers and duties of his office.

Amendment XXVI.
[Proposed 1971; Ratified 1971]

Section 1. The right of citizens of the United States, who are eighteen years of age or older, to vote shall not be denied or abridged by the United States or by any State on account of age.

Section 2. The Congress shall have power to enforce this article by appropriate legislation.

Amendment XXVII.
[Proposed 1789; Ratified 1992]

No law, varying the compensation for the services of the Senators and Representatives, shall take effect, until an election of representatives shall have intervened.

Unratified Amendments
[Proposed by Congress but <u>not</u> ratified by the states]

Originally proposed First Amendment in the Bill of Rights
[Proposed 1789]

After the first enumeration required by the first article of the Constitution, there shall be one Representative for every thirty thousand, until the number shall amount to one hundred, after which the proportion shall be so regulated by Congress, that there shall be not less than one-hundred Representatives, nor less than one Representative for every forty thousand persons, until the number of Representatives shall amount to two hundred; after which the proportion shall be so regulated by Congress, that there shall not be less than two hundred Representatives, nor more than one Representative for every fifty thousand persons.

Titles of Nobility
[Proposed 1810]

If any citizen of the United States shall accept, claim, receive or retain any title of nobility or honour, or shall, without the consent of Congress, accept and retain any present, pension, office or emolument of any kind whatever, from any emperor, king, prince or foreign power, such person shall cease to be a citizen of the United States, and shall be incapable of holding any office of trust or profit under them, or either of them.

The Slavery Amendment
[Proposed 1861]

No amendment shall be made to the Constitution which will authorize or give to Congress the power to abolish or interfere, within any State, with the domestic institutions thereof, including that of persons held to labor or service by the laws of said State.

Child Labor
[Proposed 1926]

Section 1. *The Congress shall have power to limit, regulate, and prohibit the labor of persons under eighteen years of age.*

Section 2. *The power of the several States is unimpaired by this article except that the operation of State laws shall be suspended to the extent necessary to give effect to legislation enacted by the Congress.*

The Equal Rights Amendment
[Proposed 1972; Expired unratified 1982]

Section 1. *Equality of rights under the law shall not be denied or abridged by the United States or by any State on account of sex.*

Section 2. *The Congress shall have the power to enforce, by appropriate legislation, the provisions of this article.*

Section 3. *This amendment shall take effect two years after the date of ratification.*

Statehood for Washington, D.C.
[Proposed 1978; Expired unratified 1985]

Section 1. *For purposes of representation in the Congress, election of the President and Vice President, and article V of this Constitution, the District constituting the seat of government of the United States shall be treated as though it were a State.*

Section 2. *The exercise of the rights and powers conferred under this article shall be by the people of the District constituting the seat of government, and as shall be provided by the Congress.*

Section 3. *The twenty-third article of amendment to the Constitution of the United States is hereby repealed.*

Section 4. *This article shall be inoperative, unless it shall have been ratified as an amendment to the Constitution by the legislatures of three-fourths of the several States within seven years from the date of its submission.*

Appendix B:
Overview of Amendments to the Constitution

	Ratified	Major Topic	
I.	1791	Expression	
II.	1791	Weapons	
III.	1791	Housing soldiers	*Basic liberties*
IV.	1791	Privacy	
V.	1791	Rights of accused	
VI.	1791	Trial rights	
VII.	1791	Civil juries	*Due process*
VIII.	1791	Punishment	
IX.	1791	Unnamed rights	
X.	1791	Unnamed powers	
XI.	1795	Suing another state	
XII.	1804	Presidential running mates	
XIII.	1865	Slavery	*Reconstruction Amendments*
XIV.	1868	Equal protection	
XV.	1870	Voting	
XVI.	1913	Income tax	*Progressive Era Amendments*
XVII.	1913	Senate elections	
XVIII.	1919	Prohibition	
XIX.	1920	Women's suffrage	
XX.	1933	Federal office schedule	
XXI.	1933	End of prohibition	
XXII.	1951	Presidential term limits	
XXIII.	1961	Electors for Washington	
XXIV.	1964	Poll tax	
XXV.	1967	Replacing a president	
XXVI.	1971	Voting age	
XXVII.	1992	Congress' pay	

Appendix C:
Legislative Bodies and Heads of Government and State in the U.S., the U.K. and Germany

Upper House

	Number of members	Term length	Election type
United States Senate	100	6 years	Direct election
British House of Lords	760 (approx.)	life	Appointed by the monarch, by the church, or inherited
German Bundesrat	69	varies	Appointed by state governments

Lower House

	Number of members	Term length	Election type
United States House of Representatives	435	2 years	Direct election
British House of Commons	650 (approx.)	5 years	Direct election
German Bundestag	622	4 years	Direct election

Head of Government / State

	Term length	Election type	Role
U.S. President	4 years	Indirect (by elected state delegates)	Enforces law and leads policy (executive), represents nation (= British Prime Minister + Queen)
British Prime Minister	5 years	Appointed by the monarch (leader of majority party in the Commons)	Leads House of Commons (legislative), represents the Queen (executive) (= U.S. President + Speaker of the House)
British Monarch	life	Inherited	Represents UK and Commonwealth, governs through Prime Minister and Parliament
German Chancellor	4 years	Chosen by President and Bundestag	Leads Bundestag, executes policy with its support (legislative and executive)
German Federal President	5 years	Appointed by convention	Ceremonial head of state, government supervisor

Index of Selected Topics

Articles of Confederation, *3-4*, 5, 7, 9, 12, 16, 27, 31, 46, 57f, 65, 70, 84
Bill of Rights, 3, 13, *74*, 85, 91, 93, 94, 98, *99-100,* 101, 107, 119, 132-133
Back Civil Rights Movement, 109, 113, 125, 128
commerce clause, *32-34*, 129, 135
citizenship, 9, 11, 13, 32, *35*, 44, 61-62, 66, 76, *90*, *107-111*, 116, *98-100*, 101-113, 116, 121, 127-128, 131, 133
civil rights, 100, 102, 107-109, 121, 127-129
Civil War, 10, 13, 39, 67, 101, *104*, 106, 112, 131
drug laws, 26, 71, 89
executive orders, 56-57, 64, 104
free press, 82, 83
gun law, *84-87*, 92, 119
health care, 20-21, 33-34
juries, 63, *91-97*, 98, 108-109
Native Americans (Indians), 19, 32, 79-89, 100, 107, 111, 116
political parties, 26-27, 28, 50, 127
presidential elections, *46-50*, 102-103, 121, 122-123, 125-126, 127
privacy rights, *87-90*, 93, 99, 110
religion, 72-73, *76-81*, 110, 116
racial violence, 87, 92
same-sex marriage, 66, 81, 110
slavery, 3, *8-11*, 14, 19, 33, 41-42, 66, 100-101, *103-110*, 111, 113, 133, 167
Supreme Court decisions,
- historic, 63, 71-72, 79, 96, 102, 109, 127-129
- recent 33-34, 42, 56, 64, 66, 81, 83, 85, 94-95, 98-99, 110
terrorism, 83-84, 88-90, 93-94, 98
voting rights, 18, 47, 100-101, *111-113*, 114-116, *120-122*, *127-129*, *131-133*
women's rights, 18, 71, 80, 101, 110, 111, 116, *120-122*

About the Author

Lucas Kent Ogden, a native of northern California, has taught numerous courses related to American legal issues for European university students, business people, and government workers. He is now a lecturer on American constitutional law at the University of Tübingen in southwestern Germany. In Tübingen, he also regularly speaks and presents on various topics for the German-American Institute, and gives historical city tours. Ogden completed his bachelor's degree in Chico, California, and an advanced degree in theology (*Magister der Theologie*) in Tübingen, where he is currently working on his dissertation. He also studied in Mainz (Germany), Strasbourg (France), and Basel (Switzerland). As a speaker and instructor, Ogden is known for his clear and engaging approach.